CLIL

Discuss the Changing World 2

Miyako Nakaya   Miyuki Yukita
Masaru Yamazaki   Bill Benfield

SEIBIDO

参考図書

UNIT 3
『脱プラスチック　データで見る課題と解決策』 日経ナショナルジオグラフィック社 2021
チャールズ・モア, カッサンドラ・フィリップス著, 海輪由香子訳 『プラスチックスープの海　北太平洋巨大ごみベルトは警告する』NHK出版 2012

UNIT 6
アンドレア・ウォーレン著, もりうちすみこ訳 「十歳、ぼくは突然「敵」とよばれた」汐文社 2019

UNIT 9
青木健太著 「タリバン台頭」 岩波書店　2022
岡部芳彦著 「本当のウクライナ」 ワニブックス　2022
増田雅之編著 「ウクライナ戦争の衝撃」 インターブックス　2022

UNIT 10
堤未果著 「デジタル・ファシズム」 NHK出版新書 2021
伊藤亞聖著 「デジタル化する新興国」中公新書 2020

UNIT 12
広原盛明著 「観光立国政策と観光都市京都：インバウンド、新型コロナに翻弄された京都観光」 文理閣　2020
上山肇, 須藤廣, 増淵敏之編著 「ポストマスツーリズムの地域観光政策：新型コロナ危機以降の観光まちづくりの再生へ向けて」 公人の友社 2021

UNIT 13
エリン・メイヤー著 「異文化理解力」英治出版　2015
Meyer, E. (2015). The Culture Map. PUBLICAFFAIRTS: New York
千葉祐大著 「異文化理解の問題地図」技術評論社 2019
鳥飼久美子著「異文化コミュニケーション学」 岩波書店 2021

UNIT 14
椿進著「超加速経済アフリカ」東洋経済 2021
白戸圭一著 「アフリカを見る　アフリカから見る」 ちくま新書 2019

音声ファイルのダウンロード／ストリーミング

CDマーク表示がある箇所は、音声を弊社HPより無料でダウンロード／ストリーミングすることができます。下記URLの書籍詳細ページに音声ダウンロードアイコンがございますのでそちらから自習用音声としてご活用ください。

http://seibido.co.jp/ad666

CLIL : Discuss the Changing World 2

は し が き

　本書は、2020年に出版された "Discuss the Changing World" の第2弾です。このテキストの最終目標は、「自分の意見」を言えるようになることです。日常の事柄でも、政治経済についての事柄でも、自分がどのような意見をもっているのかを伝えることが、コミュニケーションの大きな成果となります。そのためには、まず、話す内容についての知識を得て、自分なりの視点を見つけることが必要です。さらに、自分の考えを表現できる言語（ここでは英語）を習得することも必要です。

　本書では、この目標を成し遂げるために、CLIL（Content and Language Integrated Learning）のアプローチを使います。このテキストの中で学ぶ内容は、最新の国内外のトピックです。今まさに世界で起こっていることを学び、その問題について考えながら、英語という言語も身に着けていきます。本書の活動は、以下の通りになっています。

Listening ……………………………………… トピックについて知る
　Meaning of the key phrases ………… 語彙やフレーズを知る
　Talk about these pictures ……………… リスニングの内容を自分で語る
Reading ……………………………………… トピックについてさらに情報を得る
　Outline …………………………………… リーディングの内容を整理する
　Comprehension questions ……………… リーディングの内容理解を確認する
Translating key phrases ………………… 使えるフレーズを確実に習得する
Reading Data A and B …………………… 関連するデータを読み、伝え方を知る
Sharing Your Thoughts ………………… トピックについて自分の考えをまとめる
　Conversation ……………………………… 会話例で自分以外の考え、意見にふれる
Group Research …………………………… 協働学習でさらに情報を増やし、発信する

　トピックは、The Pandemics, The Circular Economy, Online Education, Delivery Robots, Racial Discriminationなどです。学習者のみなさんが、自分なりの興味を持って、取り組むことを期待します。

　出版にあたっては、田村栄一氏をはじめ、成美堂の皆様から、貴重なご意見やご助言をいただきました。心からお礼を申し上げます。

2022年10月

著者一同

CONTENTS

テキストでは様々な分野の15トピックを扱っています。興味のあるトピックを選んで、そこから始めてみましょう。ここでは以下のトピックを例にして、自分の意見を伝えるステップを説明します。

Topic: Healthy Food – Bananas

Introduction

A Listening

トピックに関してのニュースを聞きましょう。空欄には、数字、トピックのキーワード、一般的な重要語句、聞き取りにくい語彙などが入ります。

B Keywords and phrases

前のリスニングに出てきた単語やフレーズです。辞書で調べ、日本語の意味を確認しましょう。トピックについて話をするときに役に立つ単語やフレーズです。

C Three pictures

リスニングに関連する3つの絵です。ペアになり、それぞれの絵を英語で説明しましょう。リスニングの内容を確認し合います。

1.

2.
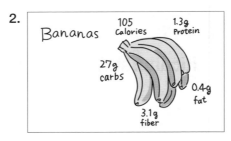

3.

1. There are three bananas. They look delicious. Bananas are nutritious, too.
2. A banana contains about 1.3 g of protein. It also contains carbs, fat, and fiber. It has 105 calories.
3. Bananas can be served sliced with cereals. The bowl can be made very quickly. Therefore, it is suitable for breakfast.

Reading

A What do you think?

ここでは、まず、トピックを通して考えてほしい質問が提示されています。学習する前に自分の意見を書いてみましょう。

例

Does eating a banana every day make people healthy?

Your answer:

Yes, I often eat bananas for breakfast. It gives me a lot of energy before I go to school.

次にパッセージが３つあります。それぞれの Title のところが抜けています。どんなタイトルが適当か、考えながら読んでみましょう。
（一人で３つ読んでもよいですし、３人グループでパッセージを一つずつ選び、あとで内容を伝え合っても構いません。）

B Choosing a good title

タイトルが複数あります。この中から最も適当なタイトルを選んで、それぞれのパッセージの最初と、下のアウトラインの最初に書き入れましょう。

C Outline

アウトラインの穴埋めをしましょう。パッセージの構成を確認することで、内容についての理解をさらに深めます。

アウトラインの形

I. タイトル（そのパラグラフの見出し）
  A. タイトルをサポートするアイデア
    1. 細かい例や説明
      a. さらに細かい例や説明

D Comprehension questions

パッセージの内容についての理解を確認します。

A Translating the Japanese sentences into English

パッセージで使われている文を例に、意見を言うときの様々な英語表現を学びます。下線の表現に注目して日本語を英訳しましょう。

Data

　　ここでは、意見をいうときに必要なエビデンス（特に図表）の伝え方について学びます。

A　トピックに関連した図表を見て、より具体的にトピックの理解を深めます。図の下にある説明文の空欄を埋めながら、図表の読み方を学び、同時に内容について理解しましょう。

B　さらにもう一つ図表を見ながら、説明の仕方を学びます。まずは図表の基本情報（タイトル、縦軸、横軸、ソースなど）を説明し、その次に、トレンド（傾向）や特徴を説明します。最後に考察がありますが、慣れてきたら自分の考えも足してみましょう。

エビデンスを入れる理由

データは、意見をサポートするエビデンス（証拠）になります。自分の意見にデータを入れることにより、説得力が増します。図表の説明に慣れてきたら、自分でエビデンスを探して意見を言うときに使ってみましょう。

エビデンスを探すときのコツ

探し方はさまざまです。インターネットで検索したり、本や、新聞・雑誌を読んだり、ニュースで見たりしたことがエビデンスになります。このときに重要なことは、情報源をしっかりと記録して、意見を言うときに提示することです。また、インターネットを読んだときは、閲覧した日付と URL を控えておきます。

説得力のある意見を言うためには、エビデンスの情報源はより信頼のおけるものが望ましいです。企業や団体、公的機関、専門家などが公的に発信しているものは、より信頼性が高いと言えるでしょう。個人のブログはできるだけ避けますが、それが専門家のものであれば説得力があるかもしれません。その情報源がどれくらい信頼性があるかを客観的に判断し、自分の意見をサポートしましょう。

Sharing Your Thoughts

A What do you think?

ここでは Reading の最初に答えた質問について、もう一度考えます。関連するパッセージを読み、データを理解したので、もっと質問について深く考えることができるようになっているはずです。より説得力のある理由などを入れて、自分の考えを伝えてみましょう。

例

Does eating a banana every day make people healthy?

Your answer:

1. Yes, according to a report, bananas are one of the world's healthiest foods.
2. They are not only nutritious but contain a variety of nutrients such as potassium, vitamin C, and folic acid.

or

1. No, bananas contain a lot of carbohydrates, and mainly sugars in ripe bananas.
2. Consuming too many bananas may lead to an increase in weight or obesity.

B Express your opinion.

ここでは会話練習をします。会話の中で自分の意見を伝えるスキルを習得しましょう。

自分の意見を言う時のストラテジー

自分の意見をどのように伝えると効果的か、ケースごとにアドバイスがあります。
Exercise で日本語を英訳して練習してみましょう。

Group Research

ここでは、トピックについて新しい観点からさらに考えます。表に合わせてさまざまな
リサーチをします。グループで担当を決めてリサーチし、わかったことを発表し合いま
しょう。最後にわかったことを英語で書いてみましょう。

各国の食育についてリサーチした場合

It is important to eat a balanced diet. We need to plan what to eat in order to
improve our health. A plan of an ideal diet can be taught at elementary schools
because a balanced diet is important for a child's development. Japan and the
U.S. try to educate children on what to eat by providing healthy eating
guidelines, for example, "a Japanese food guide spinning top" and "the healthy
eating pyramid," respectively.

Pandemic and People's Lifestyle

Introduction

1-02

A Listen to the following news story and fill in the blanks.

The Central Japan Railway Company set up ¹(   ) booths on some of its Shinkansen bullet trains in ²(   ) (   ). The "S-Work Car," which allows passengers to work easily with a PC, can be found in the No.7 car of the Nozomi super express on the Tokaido and Sanyo Shinkansen lines. The booth is a ³(   ) room that can be used for short meetings, web conferencing, or telephone calls without people having to worry about disturbing other passengers. With the increase in ICT-based ⁴(   ) due to the COVID-19 pandemic, ⁵(   ) styles are not tied to a particular place, and web conferencing is ⁶(   ). In light of this increasing demand for new ways of working, the railway company has made new efforts such as an improvement in the in-car Wi-Fi environment and the launch of this service for ⁷(   ) travelers. With the smoking ban on trains coming into force in 2020, the company replaced ⁸(   ) cars with these business booths. They are ⁹(   ) with a table, chairs, and an electrical outlet and offer a single usage time of up to ¹⁰(   ) minutes.

5

10

B The following are keywords or phrases from the listening. Look them up in your dictionary and write the meanings.

1. set up   _____
2. booth   _____
3. passenger   _____
4. web conferencing   _____
5. telework   _____
6. work styles   _____
7. be equipped with   _____

C Talk about these pictures and check your understanding of the listening.

1.
2.
3.

A What do you think?

> After the COVID-19 pandemic, will people's lives change?

Your answer: _____

•Passage 1 **Title (**)

Infectious diseases have been around since the dawn of civilization. The earliest humans lived in small isolated communities, so they had limited opportunity to share viruses. However, people began to live in larger cities, and more trade routes developed, bringing them into contact with more people.
5 Urbanization created denser neighborhoods and airline flights enabled humans to interact over wider areas. Exposure to diseases gave people some level of immunity. Better understanding of transmission led to improved sanitation, and vaccines have eliminated some diseases. In the COVID-19 pandemic, governments asked citizens to keep a certain distance from each other. People
10 also started to use digital devices for both socializing and business so that they could maintain connections without meeting each other in person.

•Passage 2 **Title (**)

When the pandemic forced people to stay at home, social and business activities were interrupted for some time. However, Zoom meetings enabled them to keep in touch. From Zoom birthdays to Zoom weddings, the video
15 conferencing tool created a safer alternative to in-person events. In December 2019, before the pandemic started, Zoom had about 10 million daily users. A year later, it had 350 million daily meeting participants. Now that pandemic restrictions have eased, people have resumed in-person events. However, they have developed new habits and have accepted that they do not need to meet
20 others face-to-face every time. Office employers plan to use a hybrid work model, where their employees can work either at the office or from home.

•Passage 3 **Title (**)

By the end of 2022, people had been wearing masks for almost three years, and an increasing number of young people in Japan have become reluctant to show their faces without a mask. They say they will continue wearing a mask.
25 According to a survey in March 2021, people are more conscious of hiding their faces than trying to prevent infection. Some say that if they wear a mask, they do not have to wear makeup. Others say that they can hide an unshaven face or make their face look smaller. Some people also think that a mask is now part of their face. They are especially reluctant to show their face to people they met
30 after the pandemic started.

B Choose a good title for each passage from the choices below.

1. Sanitation and vaccines
2. Zoom meetings after the pandemic
3. Fashionable face masks
4. Zoom birthdays and Zoom weddings
5. Hiding faces with masks
6. How humans have coexisted with infectious diseases

C Fill in the blanks and write an outline for each passage.

•Passage 1

I. _____

    A. the earliest humans

        1. small _____ communities

        2. _____ opportunities to share viruses

    B. urbanization and airline flights

        1. _____ neighborhoods

        2. _____ over wider areas

•Passage 2

I. _____

    A. Zoom meetings

        1. a _____ to in-person events

        2. _____ daily meeting participants in 2020

    B. A new way of life

        1. not needing to _____ every time

        2. a _____ work model where some workers work remotely some of the time

•Passage 3

I. _____

    A. reluctant to stop wearing masks

        1. no need to wear _____

        2. no need to _____ their face

        3. their face can look _____

D Comprehension questions

1. During the COVID-19 pandemic, what have digital devices been used for?

    _____

2. What kind of habits and ideas have people developed during the pandemic?

    _____

3. When people wear masks, what are they more conscious of?

    _____

Key phrases

A Use the following key phrases and translate the Japanese sentences into English.

例文 1

Airline flights <u>enabled</u> humans <u>to</u> interact over wider areas.

Question

ビデオ会議により自宅で勤務することが可能となった。

Answer

....

....

例文 2

A <u>year later</u>, it had 350 million daily meeting participants.

Question

一年後、学校は旅行などの行事を再開した。

Answer

....

....

例文 3

They <u>are</u> especially <u>reluctant to</u> show their face to people they met after the pandemic started.

Question

多くの人が外出することを嫌がった。

Answer

....

....

Data

 1-06

A Study the figures and fill in the blanks.

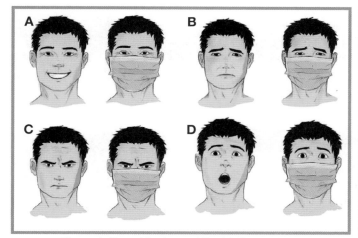

Figure 1. Face Masks and Facial Expressions

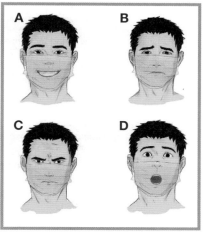

Figure 2. Transparent Face Masks

Source: Frontiers "Effect of Face Masks on Interpersonal Communication During the COVID-19 Pandemic"
https://www.frontiersin.org/articles/10.3389/fpubh.2020.582191/full

Figure 1 shows face masks and 1_____. Face masks cover the middle and the lower portions of the 2_____. Therefore, facial expressions involving the mouth, lips, teeth, and nose are masked during 3_____ communication. Picture A shows a smiley face. It is perceived when the corners of the lips rise upward. With face masks, happiness can be seen on the face by looking at the wrinkles at the edge of the 4_____. Picture B shows a sad face. Eyebrows and the corners of the lips move downward, but because of the masks, we can see only 5_____. Picture C shows anger. Its facial expression emphasizes the downward and central movement of eyebrows and the angry 6_____. We cannot see the expression from the 7_____ because they are covered by the masks. Picture D shows expressions of 8_____ and shock. They are usually formed of elevated eyebrows and a raised upper lip, but the 9_____ is covered by the masks.

As shown in Figure 2, 10_____ face masks can preserve the importance of facial expressions during interpersonal communication. By using them, different 11_____ can easily be picked up through the individual's 12_____ reactions and expressions.

B Study the figure and fill in the blanks.

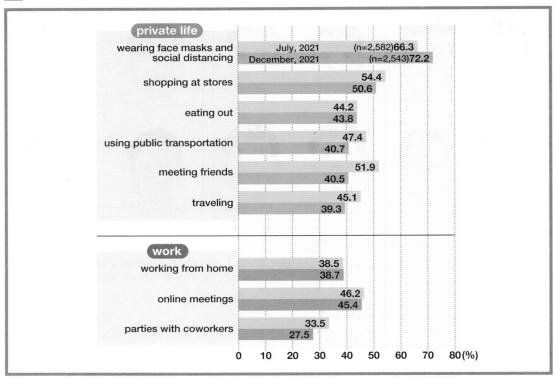

Figure 3. New Lifestyle a Year Later

Source: NLI Research Institute「新型コロナによる暮らしの変化に関する調査」より作成
https://www.nli-research.co.jp/files/topics/70768_ext_18_0.pdf?site=nli

1. Figure 3 shows how people guess about their _____ in a year's time. It shows what percentage of the respondents answered that they would do the things listed in the graph more often.

2. The survey was conducted by NLI Research Institute in _____.

3. In December 2021, _____% of the respondents said that people would continue wearing masks and social distancing.

4. More respondents agreed with this idea than in _____ 2021.

5. As for going out, _____% of the respondents said people would go shopping at stores.

6. However, the number _____ from July.

7. Also, 38.7% of them said _____.

8. Asked about working style, _____% of the respondents said the number of business trips would decrease, and people would have more online meetings.

9. Only _____% of them said people would enjoy parties with coworkers, and the number decreased from July.

Sharing Your Thoughts

A What do you think?

After the COVID-19 pandemic, will people's lives change?

Your answer:

1. _____

2. _____

3. _____

4. _____

5. _____

B Express your opinion.

 1-08

Sample conversation

A: The pandemic has continued for about three years and people have become accustomed to the new way of life. After the pandemic, do you think our lifestyle will change?

B: I don't think so. For example, we've learned how convenient online meetings are. <u>Many people</u> will continue having meetings without meeting face-to-face.

A: Do you think face-to-face communication will decrease?

B: Yes, I do. For example, parties used to be important in business for socializing, but we've got used to life without parties. <u>Many people</u> will use their time for other things.

自分の意見を言う時のストラテジー

全員一致ではなく多くの人にあてはまると思われる時は、次のような語句を主語にします。

　　Many people / Many of us, Most people / Most of us

Exercise 人々は引き続き感染防止に気をつけて、多くの人はマスクを外すことをためらうでしょう。

....

....

Group Research

1. Do some research to find how our lifestyle has been affected by the COVID-19 pandemic. Write your findings in the box below.

Examples	Effects

2. What did you think about the results of your group's research? Talk and write about them in your group.

UNIT 2

The Circular Economy

Circular Economy

Introduction

🎵 1-09

A **Listen to the following news story and fill in the blanks.**

In the Olympic and Paralympic Games in Tokyo in 2021, all the ¹( ) were
made from electronic waste such as discarded smartphones. A project to ²( )
used smartphones and other gadgets was launched in 2018. In ³( ) years,
enough gold, silver, and copper, etc. was collected to make about ⁴( ) medals.
Collecting precious and rare metals in this way is called urban mining. Research in 5
2008 estimated that the amount of gold retrievable from urban mining in Japan
accounted for ⁵( ) percent of the world's gold reserves. Collecting and extracting
these metals efficiently can prevent the ⁶( ) of limited resources. One
example is EV batteries. Because the ⁷( ) toward electric vehicles (EVs) is gaining
momentum, EV batteries eventually need to be ⁸( ). We must therefore 10
develop ways to extract and recover minerals such as lithium, nickel, and cobalt from
these ⁹( ) batteries. Recovering 100 percent of these materials and ¹⁰( )
them in new EV batteries will create a circular economy.

B **The following are keywords or phrases from the listening. Look them up in
your dictionary and write the meanings.**

1. electronic waste   _____
2. discarded smartphones   _____
3. precious and rare metals   _____
4. gold retrievable from urban mining   _____
5. world's gold reserves   _____
6. EV batteries   _____
7. extract and recover minerals   _____
8. a circular economy   _____

C **Talk about these pictures and check your understanding of the listening.**

1.

2.

3.
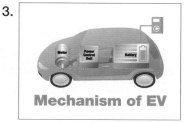

Mechanism of EV

A What do you think?

> **What are the difficulties we may face in moving to a circular economy?**

Your answer: _____

•**Passage 1 Title (   )**

   A circular economy refers to an economy where all products such as metal, plastic, and fabric are recycled with minimum additional new resources being used. It is not a linear economy where items are produced, consumed, and disposed of. On the contrary, products are designed to last a long time and can be repaired easily. When they cannot be used anymore, they are recycled to produce new products or buried in a landfill if biodegradable. Therefore, products should be carefully designed to fit this cycle. For example, smartphones should be easy to break down into parts so that precious metals and rare metals can be collected and recycled easily. In this way, resources will not run out, helping to create a sustainable society.

•**Passage 2 Title (   )**

   Subscription is one way to reuse products. It is a system where people share products such as cars, clothes, and toys rather than own them. People pay when they use them and give them back when they are finished. For example, cars are parked most of the time. If these cars are shared, people can maximize the rate of car operation and minimize car production. This will save resources and energy. Moreover, automakers will have a reason to make more durable cars which will suit this system. Likewise, by using subscription, children can share a variety of toys with others. Children's interest in particular toys changes dramatically as they get older. Instead of buying new toys and getting rid of old ones, parents can choose to reuse toys through subscription.

•**Passage 3 Title (   )**

   Recycling is the core of a circular economy. According to the Ministry of the Environment, Japan's recycling rate was about 20% in 2019 while about 80% of trash was incinerated. Osaki, a small town in Kagoshima, achieved an 83.4% recycling rate and no incineration of trash. The local people have been sorting their trash into 27 categories for more than 20 years. For example, paper trash alone is separated into eight categories such as shredded paper, copier paper, and flyers. Used cooking oil is also collected to make biodiesel fuel. The slogan of the town is "if mixed, waste is waste, if sorted and separated, it becomes a resource!" For the residents, washing used plastic bags and paper cartons before recycling has become part of their daily routine.

B **Choose a good title for each passage from the choices below.**

1. How interest in toys changes as children grow
2. The definition and system of a circular economy
3. The current situation of trash recycling in Japan
4. Reasons why people sort and separate trash
5. The issues of product design
6. Reusing products through subscription

C **Fill in the blanks and write an outline for each passage.**

•Passage 1

I. _____

   A. Definition

      1. All products are _____ with minimum additional new resources used

   B. Design of the products

      1. A careful design to fit the cycle is needed

         a. Smartphones should be designed so that _____ can be collected easily

•Passage 2

I. _____

   A. The system of subscription

      1. Sharing but not _____ products

   B. Examples

      1. Subscription for cars will save resources and energy

         a. by maximizing the _____ rate

         b. by minimizing car _____

         c. by producing more _____ cars

      2. Subscription for _____ also saves resources and energy

•Passage 3

I. _____

   A. Recycling rate of Japan

      1. about _____% of trash recycled while _____% incinerated

   B. Osaki Town in Kagoshima

      1. Achieved an _____% recycling rate and no _____ of trash

      2. The local people sort waste into _____ categories

D **Comprehension questions**

1. What is needed to create a circular economy in terms of product design?

_____

2. What are the good points of subscription?

_____

3. How did Osaki Town achieve its high recycling rate?

_____

Key phrases

A Use the following key phrases and translate the Japanese sentences into English.

例文 1

A circular economy <u>refers to</u> an economy where all products such as metal, plastic, and fabric are recycled with minimum additional new resources being used.

Question

貴金属とは、金、銀、白金などの貴重な金属のことを指す。

- 白金：platinum

Answer

例文 2

<u>Likewise</u>, by using subscription, children can share a variety of toys with others.

Question

同様に、私たちは電気自動車の燃料電池を作るために希少金属をリサイクルする必要がある。

Answer

例文 3

According to the Ministry of the Environment, Japan's recycling rate was about 20% in 2019 <u>while</u> about 80% of trash was incinerated.

Question

ゴミの分別は簡単と思う人がいる一方で、時間がかかり過ぎると思う人もいる。

- ゴミの分別：sorting and separating trash

Answer

Data 1-13

A Study the figure and fill in the blanks.

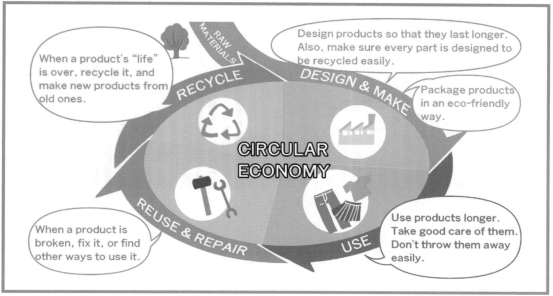

Figure 1. The System of a Circular Economy

Source: National Geographic kids. より作成
https://www.natgeokids.com/uk/discover/science/general-science/all-about-the-circular-economy/

Figure 1 shows the system of a circular economy. The arrows show the four stages:
1_____, 2_____, 3_____, and 4_____.
Altogether, the arrows show a closed circle. The speech bubbles show the directions for
each stage.

In the "DESIGN & MAKE" stage, you can see a picture of a 5_____. The
products produced here need to be designed to 6_____ longer and 7_____ easily.
They also need to be packaged in an 8_____ way.

The next stage is the "USE" stage. The picture here shows 9_____. In a circular
economy, people need to use a product 10_____ and try not to 11_____ it away
easily.

The third stage is "REUSE & REPAIR." The picture here shows a wrench and a
12_____. It represents the action of 13_____ the product. Here, products can be
fixed or given another use. In this way, people can use the product longer.

The last stage is "RECYCLE." The mark shows the universal recycling symbol.
Creating new products from 14_____ ones is what you need to do when the product's
"life" is over.

B Study the figure and fill in the blanks.

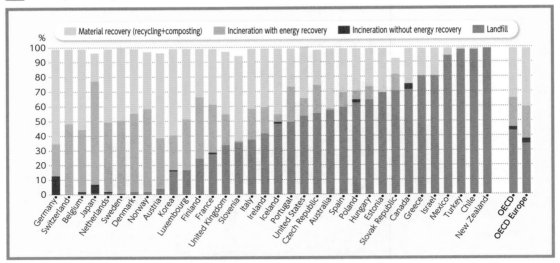

Figure 2. Municipal Waste Disposal and Recovery Shares, 2013 or Latest

Source: Environment at a Glance 2015: OECD Indicators. Municipal waste
https://read.oecd-ilibrary.org/environment/environment-at-a-glance-2015/municipal-waste_9789264235199-14-
en#page2

1. Figure 2 shows municipal waste _____ shares, 2013 or latest.

2. It shows the breakdown of how waste was finally disposed of or recovered.

3. Recovery was done in forms such as recycling, _____, and generating energy in incineration.

4. The vertical axis shows the percentage of the four disposal and recovery types of municipal waste, which are _____, incineration with energy recovery, incineration without energy recovery, and _____.

5. The horizontal axis shows 34 _____ countries including Japan.

6. The country which had the highest share of its waste in landfills was _____ at 100%.

7. The country that had the highest share of its waste in material recovery was _____ at 65%.

8. Japan had the highest share of its waste in _____ at 71%.

9. This means that Japan _____ most of its waste and generated energy from it.

10. Compared to other OECD countries, Japan's municipal waste can also be characterized by hardly being put into _____.

Sharing Your Thoughts

A What do you think?

> **What are the difficulties we may face in moving to a circular economy?**

Your answer:

1. _____

2. _____

3. _____

4. _____

5. _____

B Express your opinion.

 1-15

Sample conversation

A: A circular economy is ideal in creating a sustainable and ecological society, but I think there are a lot of difficulties that we must overcome here.

B: I think so, too. I've seen people in Osaki Town washing used plastic bags and hanging them to dry. It seemed quite tough to do that every day. <u>I wonder</u> if there are much easier ways to recycle plastic.

A: Well, once people get used to it, it might not be a problem. I rather worry about the high cost for changing the designs of products. This will affect every existing manufacturing line.

B: I think innovation always comes with burdens. It's time we face it and think about protecting the environment seriously. I've heard that crude oil and natural gas will last only another 50 years if we keep consuming them at the present speed. <u>I wonder</u> what will happen if we don't make a change now.

自分の意見を言う時のストラテジー

意見を言う時に、これに関してはどうなのだろう、と疑問に思うポイントが出てくることがあります。そのようなときは、I wonder を使って、そのポイントが気がかりだ、あるいは、そのポイントに気づいていることを相手に伝えてみましょう。

　　I wonder if there are much easier ways to recycle plastic.

Exercise その焼却炉が有害物質を排出することはないのかどうか疑問です。

● 焼却炉：incinerator　● 有害物質：toxic substances

Group Research

1. Do some research to find companies that offer products and services that support a circular economy. Write your findings in the box below.

Name of the company	(The LEGO Group)	(Patagonia)	
The product or service of the company			
Who the targeted customers are			
Where the targeted customers are			
How the product or service fit the circular economy			
Details			

2. What did you think about the results of your group's research? Talk and write about them in your group.

UNIT 3

Road to Decarbonization

Introduction

A **Listen to the following news story and fill in the blanks.**

The NISSIN FOODS Group began using the [1]( ) ECO Cup in December [2]( ). It is designed to protect the environment and make effective use of [3]( ). The company also intends to [4]( ) CO_2 emissions in its business activities. The company is promoting the use of the biomass plastic, which contributes to resource [5]( ). Cup Noodle, the world's first instant noodles in a cup, was released in 1971 and it was initially [6]( ) in foamed polystyrene cups, but in 2008, the company began to use paper, a [7]( ) resource, to reduce the amount of plastic used. In 2019, the company began switching to the biomass cups, which [8]( ) the plastic used in the cup with biomass plastic. It enabled the company to almost halve the amount of petrochemical-derived [9]( ) used per cup, and achieved a 16% reduction in CO_2 emissions. And all Cup Noodles brand products will be [10]( ) within fiscal 2022.

5

10

B **The following are keywords or phrases from the listening. Look them up in your dictionary and write the meanings.**

1. biomass _____
2. CO_2 emissions _____
3. resource circulation _____
4. foamed polystyrene _____
5. recyclable _____
6. petrochemical-derived _____
7. reduction _____

C **Talk about these pictures and check your understanding of the listening.**

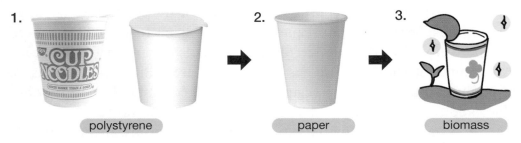

1. polystyrene   2. paper   3. biomass

A What do you think?

Do you think we should stop using plastic bags in our daily lives?

Your answer: _____

•Passage 1 **Title (   )**

　Microplastics are tiny plastic particles often found in the oceans. They result from the breakdown of larger plastic items such as water bottles. This breakdown is mainly caused by exposure to the sun's radiation and ocean waves. Microplastics are not easy to break down and take hundreds or thousands of
5 years to decompose. In the oceans, they are often eaten by marine animals, such as fish and whales. This pollution is the result of storms, water runoff, and winds that carry plastic into the oceans. Single-use plastics such as plastic bags are the primary source of this. Microplastics are also detected in seafood, and even in drinking water. They are harmful to the environment including animals and
10 humans.

•Passage 2 **Title (   )**

　Almost all plastic is derived from materials made from fossil fuels, mostly oil and gas. In the process of extracting and transporting those fuels and manufacturing plastic, greenhouse gases are produced. A lot of plastic products are discarded after a single use, and a large amount of plastic goes to landfills or
15 is incinerated, emitting greenhouse gases. Plastic waste used to be shipped to countries like China, Myanmar, and Cambodia to be handled there. However, incineration in those developing nations was poorly regulated, and greenhouse gas emissions posed considerable threats to the environment. Reducing plastic use and waste is a key to curb greenhouse gas emissions, which are accelerating
20 climate change and making the Earth warmer.

•Passage 3 **Title (   )**

　Decarbonization is the reduction of carbon dioxide emissions produced by the burning of fossil fuels. Its purpose is to lower the output of greenhouse gases into the atmosphere. Since most plastic is made from fossil fuels, we need to think about how to decarbonize plastic and cut its carbon footprint. Now
25 environmentally friendly plastic has begun to be used. Biomass plastic is made from biomass sources such as vegetable oils and corn starch, and it does not produce additional carbon dioxide, realizing carbon neutrality. Biodegradable plastic can be decomposed by the action of living organisms. It can naturally be returned to the Earth, so it does not put a burden on the environment.

B **Choose a good title for each passage from the choices below.**

1. Single-use plastics   **2.** What are microplastics?
3. Decarbonizing plastic   **4.** Fossil fuels and greenhouse gases
5. Plastic and climate change   **6.** What is a carbon footprint?

C **Fill in the blanks and write an outline for each passage.**

•Passage 1

I. _____

   A. Definition

      1. tiny _____ often found in the oceans

   B. Problems

      1. not easy to _____ and take many years to _____

      2. eaten by _____

      3. _____ are the primary source

•Passage 2

I. _____

   A. _____ are produced

      1. considerable _____ to the environment

      2. greenhouse gas emissions are accelerating _____

•Passage 3

I. _____

   A. Definition

      1. the reduction of _____ emissions produced by the _____
        of fossil fuels

   B. Environmentally friendly plastic

      1. _____ plastic is made from _____ and _____

      2. _____ plastic can be decomposed by the action of
        _____

D **Comprehension questions**

1. What is the primary source of microplastics in the oceans?

_____

2. What is most of the plastic made from?

_____

3. How is biomass plastic environmentally friendly?

_____

Key phrases

A Use the following key phrases and translate the Japanese sentences into English.

例文 1

They <u>result from</u> the breakdown of larger plastic items.

Question

気候変動は大気中への温室効果ガスの放出の結果である。

Answer

例文 2

Greenhouse gas emissions <u>pose considerable threats to</u> the environment.

Question

マイクロプラスチックは海の生態系にかなりの脅威をもたらす。

Answer

例文 3

Plastic <u>is made from</u> fossil fuels.

Question

バイオプラスチックは植物から作られる。

Answer

Data

 1-20

A Study the figure and fill in the blanks.

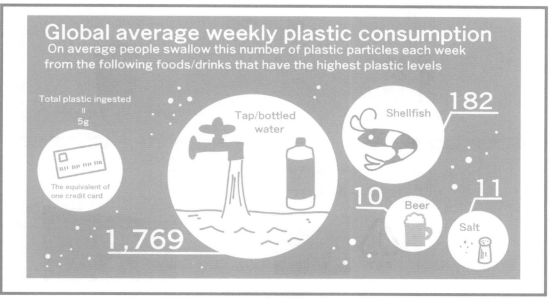

Figure 1. Global Average Weekly Plastic Consumption

Source: World Wide Fund for Nature "Estimated microplastics ingested through consumption of common foods and beverages" より作成

https://awsassets.panda.org/downloads/plastic_ingestion_press_singles.pdf

Figure 1 shows 1_____.
The source of this figure is 2_____. An
average person could be ingesting approximately 3_____ grams of plastic every week
depending on consumption habits. It is the equivalent weight of one 4_____
_____. A study by the University of Newcastle, Australia, takes a closer look at the 5
data on what plastic pollution means for human nutrition. The study estimates the
average amount of 5_____ ingested by humans. The results confirm concerns
over the large quantity of plastic we ingest every day. The study looked at plastic
consumption through food and beverages. It highlighted a list of common food and
beverages containing 6_____, such as drinking water, 7_____, 10
shellfish, and 8_____. The largest source of plastic ingestion is 9_____
with 10_____ particles of plastic. Another key source is 11_____ with
12_____ particles of plastic. This comes from the fact that they are eaten by other
sea creatures.

B Study the figure and fill in the blanks.

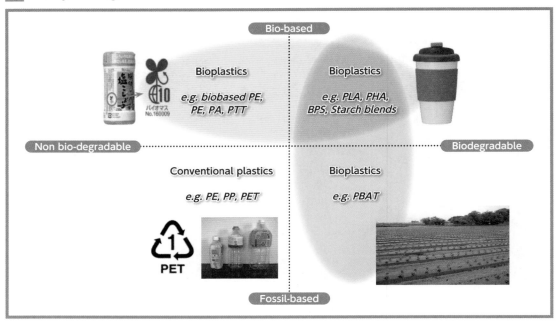

Figure 2. Comparing Four Categories of Plastic

Source: World Wide Fund for Nature "WWF Position: Biobased and Biodegradable Plastic" より作成
https://files.worldwildlife.org/wwfcmsprod/files/Publication/file/5tm1hfp3vz_WWF_Position_Biobased_and_
Biodegradable_Plastic.pdf?_ga=2.71541267.166534822.1664038939-147321265.1664038939

1. Figure 2 shows _____.

2. The source is _____.

3. The four categories are _____
    _____.

4. Two types of them are environmentally friendly. They are _____ plastics and
    _____ plastics.

5. _____ plastics are made from biomass sources. House Foods Group Inc.
    started to use them for _____ of its products.

6. _____ plastics can be decomposed by the action of living organisms.
    For example, they are used in films for _____.

7. Conventional plastics such as PET bottles are not environmentally friendly because
    they are _____ and _____.

8. Not all bio-based plastics are _____ and not all biodegradable plastics
    are _____.

9. Some of them are both _____ and _____. Starbucks sells
    _____ made from PLA plastic.

Sharing Your Thoughts

A What do you think?

> **Do you think we should stop using plastic bags in our daily lives?**

Your answer:

1. _____

2. _____

3. _____

4. _____

5. _____

B Express your opinion.

 1-22

Sample conversation

A: We've learned that plastic is bad for the environment, so we should stop using plastic bags.

B: That may be true, but I don't think it's realistic. We already have a lot of plastic bags at home. Instead of throwing them away, we can use them again and again.

A: <u>What you want to say is</u> we can reduce the number of single-use plastic bags by doing this.

B: You're right. We can reuse plastic bags. Plastic bags are light and strong, and they're also easy to carry, so they're very useful. I think avoiding single-use products is something all of us can do easily in our daily lives.

自分の意見を言う時のストラテジー

What you want to say is…という表現を使って、自分の意見を言う前に、相手の意見を自分の言葉で言い換えて確認することができます。相手の意見をよく理解してから、それに対する自分の意見を伝えることが大切です。

What you want to say is we can reduce the number of single-use plastic bags by doing this.

Exercise あなたの言いたいことは、私たちはコンビニで新しいレジ袋をもらうのをやめるべきだということですね。

....

....

---

1. Do some research to find alternatives to conventional plastic products. Write your findings in the box below.

Item	Shop	Price	Good points

2. What did you think about the results of your group's research? Talk and write about them in your group.

Online Learning and School Life

Introduction

1-23

A Listen to the following news story and fill in the blanks.

The Japanese government is planning to ease the upper limit on the number of [1](   ) that university students can take through online classes. The Ministry of Education, Culture, Sports, Science and Technology is considering introducing this change in April [2](   ). [3](   ) classes were introduced widely in Japan in the spring of 2020 in response to the outbreak of COVID-19. The biggest advantage of 5 remote learning over the traditional face-to-face approach is that it allows students to take classes anytime and [4](   ). Currently, students are allowed to take up to [5](   ) credits out of 124 required for graduation through online courses. However, the [6](   ) levels of online classes vary widely, and many students are not contented with their classes. They have been complaining about mental and physical 10 health problems due to their [7](   ) and stress from being unable to have [8](   ) communication with their classmates. Also, some students are still struggling to [9](   ) to online learning. The proposed relaxation must be done without [10](   ) the quality of education.

B The following are keywords or phrases from the listening. Look them up in your dictionary and write the meanings.

1. ease _____
2. upper limit _____
3. remote learning _____
4. be contented with _____
5. complain about _____
6. relaxation _____
7. quality of education _____

C Talk about these pictures and check your understanding of the listening.

1.

2.

卒業　単位

3.

A What do you think?

> After the COVID-19 pandemic, should universities and high schools continue promoting online learning?

Your answer: _____

•Passage 1 **Title (   )**

On February 27, 2020, the Prime Minister asked schools to close in order to contain the COVID-19 outbreak. As a result, students in Japan did not go to school for more than a month. In order to continue teaching, schools needed to give classes online. Some schools provided tablet computers for all the students, and teachers used these to give students video lessons. Students were expected to complete their homework and send it to their teachers. In this way, teachers tried to encourage them to continue learning. However, this change came suddenly, and no one had ever experienced a similar situation. Teachers and students were not ready and they felt uneasy because they did not know how long it would continue.

•Passage 2 **Title (   )**

Online classes are conducted remotely by using electronic communication. The video conferencing system allows students to attend classes online. Students do not have to be present in the classroom, so it does not matter how far the school is located from their home. All they need is a device and a stable Internet connection. Since not all students have their own computers, teachers utilize platforms that can be easily accessed with smartphones. Many high school teachers say online learning is not a complete alternative to the traditional classroom but a way to enhance it. Tasks, such as reading articles or watching videos can be done online, freeing up time for activities that require face-to-face interaction such as group work and discussion.

•Passage 3 **Title (   )**

Some students are fed up with only being offered online courses due to the COVID-19 pandemic. A university student sued his university for the return of school fees. He accused the university of not fulfilling its obligation to offer face-to-face learning opportunities for more than a year. He said there were no opportunities to make friends to talk to and the university did not adequately explain its decision, which created a sense of distrust. According to a survey, as of October 2020 more than half of the classes at universities in Japan were still online, and less than 10% of the schools said that most of their students were satisfied with this style of tuition.

B Choose a good title for each passage from the choices below.

1. COVID-19 outbreak
2. Students' frustration
3. School shutdown
4. Stable Internet connection
5. Digital access
6. The effects of online classes

C Fill in the blanks and write an outline for each passage.

•Passage 1

I. _____

    A. Schools were closed

        1. students didn't go to _____

        2. continue _____

    B. Online lessons

        1. _____ computers were provided

        2. _____ is sent to teachers

•Passage 2

I. _____

    A. Education done remotely

        1. video _____ system

        2. only a _____ and stable _____ are needed

    B. Not a complete alternative

        1. _____ can be done online

        2. free up time for activities requiring _____

•Passage 3

I. _____

    A. A university student _____

        1. not offer _____ opportunities

        2. offer only _____

        3. not adequately explain its _____

        4. created a sense of _____

D Comprehension questions

1. After schools were closed, how did schools continue teaching?

_____

2. What do students need for distance learning?

_____

3. Why did a university student sue his university for the return of school fees?

_____

Key phrases

A Use the following key phrases and translate the Japanese sentences into English.

例文 1

Some schools <u>provided</u> tablet computers <u>for</u> all the students.

Question

政府は被災者たちに食べ物と衣服を与えた。

- 被災者たち：victims

Answer

例文 2

The video conferencing system <u>allows</u> students <u>to</u> attend classes online.

Question

インターネットによって私たちは簡単に情報を得ることができる。

Answer

例文 3

<u>As of</u> October 2020, more than half of the classes at universities in Japan were still online.

Question

2015 年 4 月 1 日時点で、この町には 7 つの学校があった。

Answer

Data

1-27

A Study the figure and fill in the blanks.

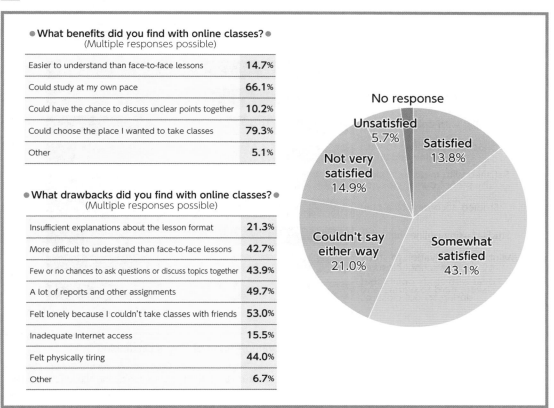

● What benefits did you find with online classes? ●
(Multiple responses possible)

Easier to understand than face-to-face lessons	**14.7%**
Could study at my own pace	**66.1%**
Could have the chance to discuss unclear points together	**10.2%**
Could choose the place I wanted to take classes	**79.3%**
Other	**5.1%**

● What drawbacks did you find with online classes? ●
(Multiple responses possible)

Insufficient explanations about the lesson format	**21.3%**
More difficult to understand than face-to-face lessons	**42.7%**
Few or no chances to ask questions or discuss topics together	**43.9%**
A lot of reports and other assignments	**49.7%**
Felt lonely because I couldn't take classes with friends	**53.0%**
Inadequate Internet access	**15.5%**
Felt physically tiring	**44.0%**
Other	**6.7%**

No response
Unsatisfied 5.7%
Satisfied 13.8%
Not very satisfied 14.9%
Couldn't say either way 21.0%
Somewhat satisfied 43.1%

Figure 1. Level of Satisfaction for Online Classes

Source: Nippon.com based on data from MEXT より作成
https://www.nippon.com/en/japan-data/h01045/

In March 2021, the Ministry of Education, Culture, Sports, Science and Technology (MEXT) conducted a survey of the effects of COVID-19 on university students' school life. Figure 1 shows the level of ₁_____ for online classes. Regarding the online classes they had taken, ₂_____% of the respondents answered that they were satisfied or ₃_____ satisfied, ₄_____% couldn't say either way, 14.9% were not very satisfied, and 5.7% were ₅_____.

When the respondents were asked about the ₆_____ of online classes, their most common response was that they could choose the ₇_____ where they wanted to take classes (79.3%). This was followed by being able to study at their own ₈_____ (66.1%). In contrast, the main ₉_____ was that students felt ₁₀_____ because they couldn't take classes with their friends (53.0%). Other common answers included that there were a lot of ₁₁_____ and other assignments (49.7%) and that classes were physically ₁₂_____ (44.0%).

B Study the figure and fill in the blanks.

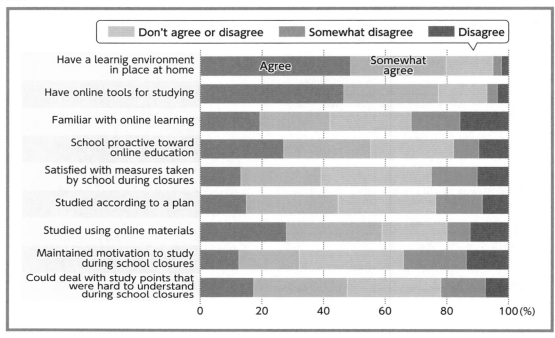

| | Don't agree or disagree | Somewhat disagree | Disagree |

- Have a learnig environment in place at home
- Have online tools for studying
- Familiar with online learning
- School proactive toward online education
- Satisfied with measures taken by school during closures
- Studied according to a plan
- Studied using online materials
- Maintained motivation to study during school closures
- Could deal with study points that were hard to understand during school closures

(scale) 0 20 40 60 80 100(%)

Agree   Somewhat agree

Figure 2. Learning Environment During Period of Social Distancing

Source: Nippon.com based on data from the Nippon Foundation "High Schoolers' Opinions on Japan's School Closures in June, 2020 A survey of Japan's 18-year-olds conducted by the Nippon Foundation"
https://www.nippon.com/en/japan-data/h00752/

1. Figure 2 shows the _____ for high school students in Japan during the school closures.

2. Around _____% of the respondents said that they had a learning environment at home.

3. They also said that they had _____ for studying.

4. _____ of the schools were proactive toward online education.

5. However, only around _____% of the students said that they were familiar with online learning.

6. Less than 40% of them said that they were _____ with the measures their school took during closures.

7. More than 30% of them said that they did not maintain _____.

8. More than 20% of them _____ according to a plan.

9. Less than half of them said that _____ difficult study points.

Sharing Your Thoughts

A What do you think?

> After the COVID-19 pandemic, should universities and high schools continue promoting online learning?

Your answer:

1. _____

2. _____

3. _____

4. _____

5. _____

B Express your opinion.

 1-29

Sample conversation

A: We've had so many online classes so far and we've learned how useful this system is. Do you think schools should promote more online learning?

B: No, I don't. I don't think schools should promote more online learning. That's because some students don't have computers at home and they have to use their smartphones. It's not easy to work on tasks with them. <u>In addition</u>, the Internet connection is not always stable at home. <u>Moreover</u>, it's not easy to keep up your motivation.

A: Doesn't your school provide tablet computers for students?

B: No. Tablet computers are available only at school and there aren't enough computers for everyone.

自分の意見を言う時のストラテジー

次の語句を使って、説明を追加することができます。

　In addition, moreover, besides, furthermore

Exercise 私はビデオで学習する授業が好きです。理由はいつでも学べることです。<u>また</u>、どこでも学べること、<u>さらに</u>、3つ目は反復して学べることです。

....

....

1. Do some research to find how the education sector in other Asian countries has been affected by COVID-19. Write your findings in the box below.
   https://equityschoolplus.jhu.edu/global-tracker/
   https://www.unicef.org/eap/covid-19-education-situation-analysis

Countries	Effects and responses	Problems
Japan		
China		
South Korea		

2. What did you think about the results of your group's research? Talk and write about them in your group.

Delivery Robots

Introduction

🎧 1-30

A **Listen to the following news story and fill in the blanks.**

We may soon see robots delivering ¹( ) and food on urban streets in Japan. In March 2021, Panasonic Holdings Corporation carried out a demonstration driving test of ²( ) robots in Fujisawa Sustainable Smart Town, Kanagawa Prefecture. More than ³( ) people live in the residential area, which has been developed as a suburban smart town utilizing information and communication ⁵ technology (ICT). In the test, two robots picked up ⁴( ) lunch boxes from a commercial facility and ⁵( ) from a pharmacy and delivered them to customers' doorsteps. In principle, the robots traveled autonomously, but they were also remotely monitored by an ⁶( ), who was standing by ready to take control in case the robots ran into any ⁷( ) operating safely. This was the first ¹⁰ time that ⁸( ) delivery robots had driven simultaneously on streets to deliver goods. Since the smart town was established in ⁹( ), Panasonic Holdings Corporation has collaborated with the local government and residents to fully harness the power of ICT in order to make life more ¹⁰( ).

B **The following are keywords or phrases from the listening. Look them up in your dictionary and write the meanings.**

1. urban streets   _____
2. a demonstration driving test   _____
3. residential area   _____
4. customers' doorsteps   _____
5. traveled autonomously   _____
6. remotely monitored   _____
7. had driven simultaneously   _____
8. fully harness   _____

C **Talk about these pictures and check your understanding of the listening.**

1.

2.

3.

A What do you think?

> What are the advantages and disadvantages of delivery robots?

Your answer: _____

•Passage 1 **Title (**)

The demand for home delivery services is rising. According to the Ministry of Land, Infrastructure, Transport and Tourism, approximately 4.8 billion packages were delivered in 2020. This was an increase of about 42 percent from 2010. The major reason for the increase is the spread of online shopping. In
5 other words, more consumers are buying goods online rather than going out and getting them. Another reason is the pandemic. One way to prevent infection is to stay at home. This decreased the flow of people while increasing that of goods. Aging is also boosting the demand for deliveries. An increasing number of old people have limited access to shopping facilities because they live in rural areas
10 or are physically weak.

•Passage 2 **Title (**)

The high demand for delivery is causing a shortage of delivery drivers, and robots can be one solution to this problem. Delivery robots have already been used inside buildings such as restaurants or hospitals. However, using them outside on the streets is still in the testing stage. The Ministry of Economy,
15 Trade and Industry set up a working group in 2019. Now the public and private sectors are cooperating closely to put delivery robots on the streets. The public sector is making laws such as those related to road traffic while the private sector is building the robots and establishing safety standards. By February 2022, tests on the streets and public roads had been carried out in 10 places.

•Passage 3 **Title (**)

20 Delivery robots made by Starship Technologies, a company founded by former Skype co-founders, can already be seen on public roads and on campuses. In the UK, the company has deployed 200 delivery robots in Milton Keynes, England. Local people come across these robots several times a day on the street, and they have become part of everyday life. The company also has a partnership
25 with the local Co-op, a member-owned supermarket. The robots deliver groceries purchased at the Co-op, charging a fee of 90 pence, or about 140 yen. In the U.S., Starship delivery robots are operating in more than 20 colleges. The average deployment is from 30 to 50 robots per college. On campus, the robots deliver food, drinks, office stationery, and other useful items for students and
30 staff.

B Choose a good title for each passage from the choices below.

1. The use of delivery robots in other countries
2. The use of delivery robots in Japan
3. The consequences of the rising demand for delivery
4. Reasons why the demand for home delivery services is increasing
5. How to build delivery robots   6. The negative impact of delivery robots

C Fill in the blanks and write an outline for each passage.

•Passage 1

  I. _____

    A. Increasing demand for delivery of food, groceries, and packages
      1. _____ packages delivered in 2020
    B. Reasons
      1. Spread of online shopping
      2. Pandemic
        a. Delivery is a way to prevent _____
      3. Aging
        a. Home delivery services help old people with limited _____ to shops

•Passage 2

  I. _____

    A. The _____ of delivery drivers
      1. Robots can solve the problem
    B. Use on streets is still in the _____ stage
      1. Working group organized by the Ministry of Economy, Trade and Industry
        a. Public sector working on making _____
        b. Private sector working on making robots and setting _____

•Passage 3

  I. _____

    A. In the UK
      1. Starship robots on the streets have become part of _____
    B. In the U.S.
      1. Starship robots are on campus delivering food and _____ stationery

D Comprehension questions

1. What are the three reasons why the demand for home delivery services is increasing?

  _____

2. What does the government need to do in order to put delivery robots on the streets?

  _____

3. What have become part of everyday life in Milton Keynes, England?

  _____

A Use the following key phrases and translate the Japanese sentences into English.

例文 1

The <u>demand for</u> home delivery services <u>is rising</u>.

Question

高齢者のために食料品を運ぶことができるロボットの需要が増えている。

• 食料品：groceries • 運ぶ：carry

Answer

例文 2

However, using them outside on the streets <u>is still in the testing stage</u>.

Question

介護ロボットの使用はまだ試験段階だ。

• 介護ロボット：nursing robots • 使用：the use

Answer

例文 3

In the UK, the company has <u>deployed</u> 200 delivery robots in Milton Keynes, England.

Question

その病院は薬を入院患者に配るために、3つの配送ロボットを配備した。

• 患者：hospitalized patients • 薬：drugs • 配る：distribute

Answer

Data

A Study the figures and fill in the blanks.

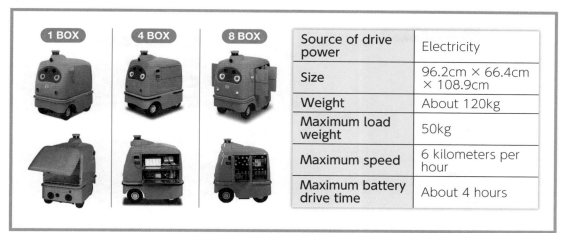

Source of drive power	Electricity
Size	96.2cm × 66.4cm × 108.9cm
Weight	About 120kg
Maximum load weight	50kg
Maximum speed	6 kilometers per hour
Maximum battery drive time	About 4 hours

1 BOX   4 BOX   8 BOX

Figure 1. Features of DeliRo

Source : ZMP INC.
https://www.zmp.co.jp/products/lrb/deliro

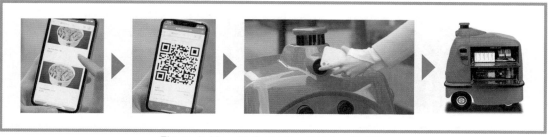

Figure 2. How to Order Food Using DeliRo

Source : ZMP INC.
https://www.zmp.co.jp/news/pressrelease_20211111

The pictures on the top show DeliRo, a delivery robot made by ZMP Inc. It was tested on the street in 2021 in Chuo Ward, Tokyo, delivering food from restaurants and convenience stores to three local condominiums. Figure 1 shows the 1_____ of DeliRo. Its length is about 2_____, width about 3_____ and height about 4_____. It comes in 5_____ types depending on what the robot delivers. The boxes are designed to carry food and daily necessities such as plastic water bottles and rice. The robot weighs about 6_____ and runs at a maximum speed of 7_____. It runs on 8_____ and can drive 9_____ hours once it is fully charged. Figure 2 shows how to order food using DeliRo. Customers can order food using an application. Once customers place an order, the app will issue a 10_____. Meanwhile, the restaurants and stores will receive the order and start preparing food. Then, DeliRo will fetch the food from the restaurant or the store and deliver it. When it arrives at the customer's front door, the customer allows DeliRo to 11_____ the QR code and the door of the container will open.

B Study the figures and fill in the blanks.

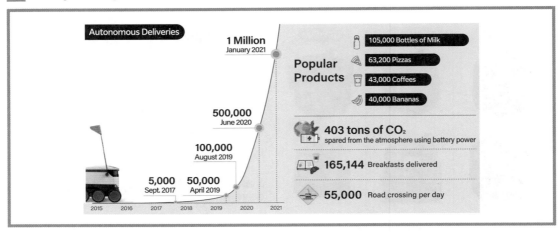

Figure 3. Accumulated Starship Deliveries Worldwide

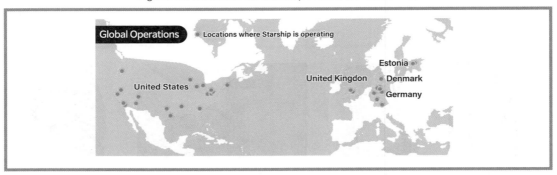

Figure 4. Global Operations of Starship

Source: Ahti Heinla. Starship Technologies. Jan 27, 2021.
https://medium.com/starshiptechnologies/one-million-autonomous-deliveries-milestone-65fe56a41e4c

1. Figure 3 shows the number of _____.

2. According to _____, the manufacturer of Starship, the number of its autonomous deliveries reached _____ in January 2021.

3. The number rocketed between _____ and January 2021 from _____ thousand to 1 million deliveries.

4. The most popular products delivered were _____ followed by _____.

5. Of the 1 million deliveries, 165,144 were delivered for _____.

6. The robots crossed roads _____ per day operating globally.

7. Figure 4 shows the _____ of Starship.

8. The robots operated in the U.S. and _____.

9. The country that had the most locations served was _____ followed by _____.

Sharing Your Thoughts

A What do you think?

> **What are the advantages and disadvantages of delivery robots?**

Your answer:

•Advantages

1. _____

2. _____

3. _____

•Disadvantages

1. _____

2. _____

3. _____

B Express your opinion.

 1-36

Sample conversation

A: Can you think of any good or bad points of delivery robots?

B: I think a good point is that they <u>can</u> ease the shortage of delivery drivers. Robots <u>can</u> work day and night without getting tired. They <u>can</u> deliver packages even late at night in response to customers' demands. What do you think?

A: I agree. They <u>can</u> also bring a sense of security to the local area, I guess. For example, they <u>can</u> say hello to children when they pass by and check if any strangers are near them. In the evening, robots <u>can</u> tell children to go home if they see them on the streets. I can picture a community with delivery robots!

B: You're right. On the contrary, I think they <u>may</u> be at risk from cyber-attacks. If robots get hacked and lose control on the street, that will be scary. Traffic accidents are another worrying point. Local people <u>may</u> get involved in the accidents, too.

> ### 自分の意見を言う時のストラテジー
>
> ポジティブな意見を言う時には助動詞の can を使えば、前向きな可能性を表現できます。逆にネガティブな意見は、助動詞の may を使えば懸念の気持ちを表すことができます。
>
> Robots <u>can</u> work day and night without getting tired.
> On the contrary, I think they <u>may</u> be at risk from cyber-attacks.
>
> **Exercise** 配達ロボットは、24時間働くことができます。なので、深夜でも宅配できます。ですが、バッテリーが切れてしまうかもしれません。
>
> ....
>
> ....

Group Research

1. Do some research to find delivery robots and their features. Write your findings in the box below.

Name of the robot	(Starship robot)	(Bellabot)	(Shonan HAKOBO)
Company that developed the robot			
The location of the headquarters			
Countries, cities, or towns where the robot is used			
Places the robot operates			
What the robot mainly delivers			
Features of the robot			

2. What did you think about the results of your group's research? Talk and write about them in your group.

UNIT 6

Discrimination against Asian Americans

Introduction

🎧 1-37

A **Listen to the following news story and fill in the blanks.**

In March, 2021, an elderly Asian American man was knocked down and ¹( ) in Oakland, California. The robber was arrested, but the man fell into a ²( ) and was declared brain-dead. On another day, a white man shot to death eight women, including six Asian Americans, in Atlanta, Georgia. Then, in September, a Japanese man was hit on the ³( ) and seriously injured by a Black man on the ⁴( ) in New York. A ⁵( ) organization called "Stop AAPI Hate" reported that from March 2020 to February 2021, there were ⁶( ) such hate crimes. The Center for the Study of Hate and Extremism at California State University also announced in a ⁷( ) that hate crimes against Asian Americans had increased by ⁸( )% in 2020 in ⁹( ) different cities in the U.S. COVID-19 may be partly ¹⁰( ) for such crimes because former president Donald Trump, among others, has called COVID-19 the "China virus." U.S. President Joe Biden ¹¹( ) Congress to pass the COVID-19 Hate Crimes Act, which he signed into law in May 2021.

5

10

(AAPI=NPO in America for opposing discrimination against Asian Americans or Pacific Islanders)

B **The following are keywords or phrases from the listening. Look them up in your dictionary and write the meanings.**

1. Asian Americans _____
2. brain-dead _____
3. shot to death _____
4. a non-profit organization _____
5. hate crimes _____
6. Hate Crimes Act _____

C **Talk about these pictures and check your understanding of the listening.**

1.
2.
3.

A What do you think?

If you were in the U.S. and experienced discrimination, what solutions could you think of?

Your answer: _____

•Passage 1 **Title (   )**

Racial discrimination against Asians started in the 19th century. During this time, a lot of Chinese people came to California to join the Gold Rush and to work on the transcontinental railroads. Slavery had been officially abolished in the U.S. in 1863. After the boom and completion of the railroads, exclusion
5 movements began because of fear that Chinese might take jobs away from Americans. In 1882, the Chinese Exclusion Act was established to prohibit Chinese workers and later Japanese workers from entering the U.S. This was the first law to restrict immigrants entering the U.S. because of their race. As a result, such racist U.S. policies limited immigrants from Asia until 1965.

•Passage 2 **Title (   )**

10 Japanese Americans have an unfortunate experience in U.S. history. Just after Japan attacked Pearl Harbor in 1941, then U.S. President Franklin D. Roosevelt signed an order to place about 120,000 Japanese Americans in 10 concentration camps, after first taking away their jobs and assets. The camps were surrounded by wire fences with armed soldiers. Additionally, Japanese
15 Americans in detention suffered from heat, cold, sand, and bugs in the deserts or the swamps where these camps were located. Although some of them fought in WWII as Americans, they were treated differently from other Asian Americans because of anti-Japanese sentiment.

•Passage 3 **Title (   )**

In 2020, various groups condemned violence against Asian Americans and
20 took action because hate crimes had become serious. These crimes included hitting and kicking, throwing stones, cutting, pushing over, setting fires, and even murder. The targets of these crimes were often the elderly, many of whom were also women. In 2021, Claire Xu, a 31-year-old Chinese American, organized a massive rally for the first time with support from many activists,
25 elected officials, and community members. A professor of Northwestern University pointed out that the younger generation was inspired by the "Black Lives Matter" protests in 2020. Encouragingly, some famous Asians in sports and culture also began to protest the violence and discrimination.

B **Choose a good title for each passage from the choices below.**

1. Actions against violence toward Asian Americans
2. The history of Asian discrimination   **3.** Chinese Americans
4. A sad experience in the U.S.   **5.** Hate crimes
6. Japanese Americans in concentration camps

C **Fill in the blanks and write an outline for each passage.**

• Passage 1

I. _____

   A. Chinese came to _____ to join the Gold Rush and to work on the transcontinental railroads.
     1. Slavery had been officially _____ in the U.S. in 1863.
   B. The Chinese Exclusion Act was established in _____.
     1. Chinese and Japanese workers were not allowed to enter the U.S. because of _____.

• Passage 2

I. _____

   A. They were detained in concentration camps after the attack on _____.
     1. Their jobs and _____ were taken away.
     2. They were surrounded by wire fences with armed soldiers.
     3. They also suffered from heat, cold, _____, and _____.
     4. Some of them fought in WWII as Americans, but they were treated differently because of _____.

• Passage 3

I. _____

   A. Various groups started to _____ the violence and took action in 2020.
     1. That's because hate crimes had gotten serious.
     2. A Chinese American organized _____.
       a. The younger generation was inspired by the _____ protests in 2020.
       b. Some famous Asians in _____ began to protest the violence.

D **Comprehension questions**

1. Why were Chinese excluded from California around 1882?

_____

2. What was taken away from Japanese Americans before they were detained in the camps?

_____

3. What incident encouraged a Chinese American to hold a rally?

_____

Key phrases

A Use the following key phrases and translate the Japanese sentences into English.

例文 1

The Chinese Exclusion Act <u>was established to</u> prohibit Chinese workers from entering the U.S.

Question

その決議が 日本人をアメリカに入れないために制定された。

- 決議：a resolution

Answer

例文 2

<u>Then</u> U.S. President Franklin D. Roosevelt signed an order.

Question

当時の菅義偉首相は、その政策に反対した。

Answer

例文 3

A Chinese American <u>organized a massive rally</u> for the first time.

Question

彼らは大規模な平和集会を東京で開催した。

Answer

Data

 1-41

A Study the figures and fill in the blanks.

	Increasing	Staying the same	Decreasing	Not sure
	81	6	2	9

Figure 1. The Percentage of Asian Adults Who Say Violence Against Asian Americans in the U.S. Is Increasing, Staying the Same, Decreasing, and Not Sure.

Experienced at least one of five incidents	45
Feared someone might threaten or physically attack them	32
People acted as if they were uncomfortable around them	27
Been subject to racial slurs or jokes	27
Someone made a remark they should go back to their home country	16
Someone made a remark that they are to blame for the coronavirus outbreak	14
Someone expressed support for them	32

*Asian adults were interviewed in English only.
Note: Figures may not add up to 100% due to rounding. No answer responses not shown.

Figure 2. The Percentage of Asian Adults Who Say Each of the Following Has Happened to Them Since the Coronavirus Outbreak Because of Their Race or Ethnicity.

Source: PEW RESEARCH CENTER "Survey of U.S. adults conducted April 5-11, 2021."
https://www.pewresearch.org/fact-tank/2021/04/21/one-third-of-asian-americans-fear-threats-physical-attacks-and-most-say-violence-against-them-is-rising

Figure 1 shows what percentage of Asian adults who say violence against them in the U.S. is 1_____, staying the same, decreasing, and not sure. Shockingly, 2_____ percent of people felt it was increasing. Figure 2 shows the 3_____ of Asian adults who say each of the following has happened to them since the coronavirus outbreak because of their race or 4_____. Forty-five percent of people experienced at least one of five incidents, and 5_____% feared someone might threaten or physically attack them. 6_____ percent of people felt that people acted as if they were 7_____ around Asians, and that they have been subject to racial 8_____ or jokes. However, it is encouraging to see that 9_____% of people have someone expressing support for them.

B Study the figure and fill in the blanks.

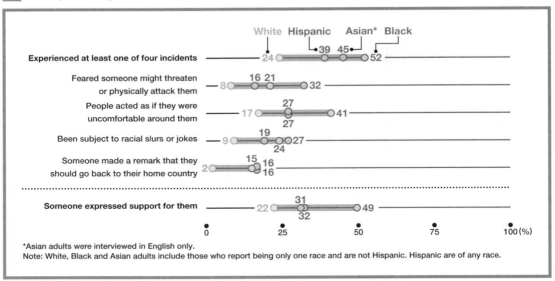

Figure 3: The Percentage of Asian, Black, Hispanic, and White Adults Saying Each of the Following Has Happened to Them Since the Coronavirus Outbreak Because of Their Race or Ethnicity

Source: PEW RESEARCH CENTER "Survey of U.S. adults conducted April 5-11, 2021."
https://www.pewresearch.org/fact-tank/2021/04/21/one-third-of-asian-americans-fear-threats-physical-attacks-and-most-say-violence-against-them-is-rising/

1. Figure 3 shows what _____ of Asian, Black, _____, and White adults saying each of the following has happened to them since the coronavirus outbreak because of their race or ethnicity.

2. The source of this data is the _____ Center.

3. After Blacks, _____ experienced the second highest number of cases in the category "experienced at least one of four incidents."

4. Interestingly, however, about _____% of Asians feared someone might threaten or physically attack them. And this was much higher than the response of _____.

5. _____ of both Asians and Hispanics experienced people acting as if they were uncomfortable around them.

6. Additionally, _____% of Asians felt they were subject to racial slurs or jokes.

7. About the same percentage of Asians, Blacks, and Hispanics experienced someone making a remark that they should go back to _____.

8. It can be said that in _____ categories, Asians had a bad experience.

Sharing Your Thoughts

A What do you think?

> If you were in the U.S. and experienced discrimination, what solutions could you think of?

Your answer:

1. _____

2. _____

3. _____

4. _____

B Express your opinion.

🎧 1-43

Sample conversation

A: Finding a solution for discrimination may be difficult for Asian Americans.

B: Why is that?

A: Partly because Asian Americans are generally considered as a model minority or successful minority, and their success stories are used to criticize Blacks and Hispanics.

B: So, what you mean is that they make enemies without realizing it. Now I understand why Chinese and Korean stores were sometimes attacked by Blacks and Hispanics although they were not a direct target of their demonstration.

A: That's right, and historians describe Asian Americans as hard-working, uncomplaining, and great achievers because they overcame a lot of hardships throughout history.

B: I see. Then, what is the main reason for the difficulty in finding a solution?

A: It's mainly because Asian Americans are divided ethnically. Even if you say Asian Americans, there are Chinese Americans, Japanese Americans, Korean Americans, Vietnamese Americans, and so on. They came to the U.S. at different times with different backgrounds. So, Asian Americans cannot be considered as one ethnic group. And it's difficult for them to take unified action.

> **自分の意見を言う時のストラテジー**
>
> 理由を言う時、部分的な理由と主な理由を分けて言うと、自分の考えをより明確に表現できます。
>
>   Partly because (of) ～ .   mainly because (of) ～ .
>
> *Exercise* 非難は、一部は彼の言動のせいですが、主には誤解のせいです。
>
> ....
>
> ....

Group Research

1. Do some research to find various regulations and measures for dealing with racial discrimination. Write your findings in the box below.

	Various regulations and measures for dealing with racial discrimination
The United Nations	
The United States	
Japan	
Ourselves	

2. What did you think about the results of your group's research? Talk and write about them in your group.

UNIT 7

Gendered Division of Housework

Introduction

🎧 1-44

A **Listen to the following news story and fill in the blanks.**

After the outbreak of COVID-19, many women ¹( ) that they had become tired of cooking. This was because many of their family members worked or studied ²( ) from home to avoid contact with others. Consequently, many women had to cook more meals for them. According to a survey ³( ) in March 2021 by Kureha, a chemical products manufacturer, of 200 dual-income couples in ₅ their ⁴( ) to ⁵( ), 70% of the wives said they cooked ⁶( ) of meals on weekdays. This shows that women do most of the cooking even though they work. Similarly, in 2020, working wives spent an average of nearly ⁷( ) hours a day on housework while working husbands spent ⁸( ) minutes, according to the Gender Equality Bureau Cabinet Office. Therefore, the office is ⁹( ) men to do ₁₀ more domestic chores. Gendered division of housework has long been an ¹⁰( ) for many countries. Even in Sweden and Norway, which are known to have gender-equal societies, women do more housework than men.

B **The following are keywords or phrases from the listening. Look them up in your dictionary and write the meanings.**

1. the outbreak of COVID-19 _____
2. dual-income couples _____
3. an average of _____
4. the Gender Equality Bureau Cabinet Office _____
5. domestic chores _____
6. gendered division of housework _____
7. gender-equal societies _____

C **Talk about these pictures and check your understanding of the listening.**

1.
2.
3.

Reading

 1-45～47

A What do you think?

> **Wives and husbands should do housework equally.**

Your answer: _____

• **Passage 1 Title (**)

   Traditionally, women have been responsible for housework while men have worked outside. This gendered division of housework is still prevalent in many households. According to family sociologists, economic power is one factor. If the breadwinner is the husband, wives often feel that it is their role to do
5 housework because they live on their partner's income. Another factor is time restriction. If wives have more time to do housework than their partners, they also accept it. Husbands' long working hours can be one of the cases. Another factor sociologists point out is traditional gender ideology. Some women feel happy to do most of the housework because of family tradition or social norms.

• **Passage 2 Title (**)

10 Many countries have adopted the policy of increasing women's employment. One reason is that the policy will promote gender equality. Universally, women have the right to work to their full potential and enjoy earning and spending money as much as men. Another is that women supporting their household economically will enrich the family in many ways. For example, children can
15 have the food and education they need. Women can also revitalize the low growth of the economy. Aging and a declining birthrate are causing a shortage of workers. If more women work, it will increase the GDP and tax revenue of the country. This will also promote the welfare of all citizens. To have more women in the workplace, a fair division of housework is necessary.

• **Passage 3 Title (**)

20 People have different ideas about gender roles, but a mismatch in the ideas can affect marital happiness. According to a group of economists (2021), in the U.S., a greater mismatch in ideas on gender roles between men and women can lead to lower marriage rates and higher divorce rates. In other words, marital happiness is likely to be lower if couples have different ideas about their roles.
25 However, a report by NHK (2015) says sharing domestic chores can be the key. Although factors that determine satisfaction in family life differed between countries, one thing that was common was that when couples shared domestic chores, satisfaction became stronger. This means that sharing domestic chores may enhance the relationship between couples.

B **Choose a good title for each passage from the choices below.**

1. Benefits of women's employment
2. Women's complaints about gendered division of housework
3. Increase of dual-income couples
4. What brings happiness in family life
5. Why women have accepted gendered division in housework
6. The future of gender-egalitarian societies

C **Fill in the blanks and write an outline for each passage.**

•Passage 1

I. _____

   A. Economic power
      1. Husbands are the _____
   B. Time restriction
      1. Wives have more _____
   C. Traditional gender ideology
      1. Wife doing housework is a family _____ or a social _____

•Passage 2

I. _____

   A. Promotion of gender equality
      1. Women's right to _____ equally with men
   B. Economic support
      1. Enrich the family
   C. Revitalization of economy
      1. Increase the _____ and _____ of a country

•Passage 3

I. _____

   A. A greater _____ in ideas on gender roles
      1. Causes lower _____ rates and higher _____ rates
   B. Sharing of domestic chores
      1. Enhances _____ between couples

D **Comprehension questions**

1. What are the three reasons why women traditionally do most of the housework?

_____

2. Why have governments adopted the policy of increasing women's employment?

_____

3. According to NHK(2015), how can couples feel satisfied with their family life?

_____

Key phrases

A Use the following key phrases and translate the Japanese sentences into English.

例文 1

This gendered division of housework is still prevalent in many households.

Question

これらの偏見は未だに東アジアの多くの家庭で広く見られる。

- 偏見：prejudices　- 家庭：households

Answer

例文 2

Many countries have adopted the policy of raising women's employment.

Question

その企業は男女共同参画の方針をとっていることで有名だ。

- 男女共同参画：gender equality

Answer

例文 3

In other words, marital happiness is likely to be lower if couples have different ideas about their roles.

Question

妻の家事参加率は夫のそれに比べて、ほとんどの国で高い傾向にある。

- 家事参加率：housework participation rate

Answer

Data

CD 1-48

A Study the figure and fill in the blanks.

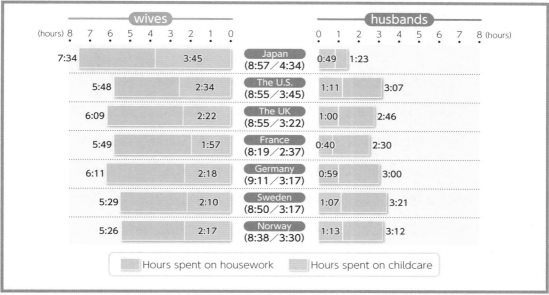

Figure 1. International Comparison of Average Numbers of Hours Spent on Housework and Childcare per Day of Couples Who Have Children Under 6 Years of Age.

Source: The white paper on gender equality 2020. Gender Equality Bureau Cabinet Office. より作成
https://www.gender.go.jp/about_danjo/whitepaper/r02/zentai/html/column/clm_01.html

Figure 1 shows an international comparison of the average number of hours spent on ₁_____ and ₂_____ per day of couples who have children under ₃_____ of age. The chart on the left shows the hours of wives, and the one on the right, those of ₄_____. The red areas of the bars show the number of hours spent on ₅_____ and the blue, on ₆_____. The total number of hours spent by both wives and husbands are shown under each country. The number on the left shows the total number of hours spent on both housework and childcare while the one on the right shows hours spent only on ₇_____. The chart was produced by the Gender Equality Bureau Cabinet Office in 2020.

Of the seven countries, Japanese wives spent the most time on housework and childcare at ₈_____ per day while Norwegian wives spent the least time at ₉_____. On the other hand, ₁₀_____ husbands spent the most time on housework and childcare at 3 hours and 21 minutes while ₁₁_____ husbands spent the least time at one hour and 23 minutes. The difference in time spent between wives and husbands was the biggest in ₁₂_____. Wives spent ₁₃_____ _____ more than husbands. In ₁₄_____, the difference was the least at 2 hours and 8 minutes. The result shows that Japanese couples who have small children spend more time on housework and childcare than other countries and the burden falls mainly on ₁₅_____.

B Study the figure and fill in the blanks.

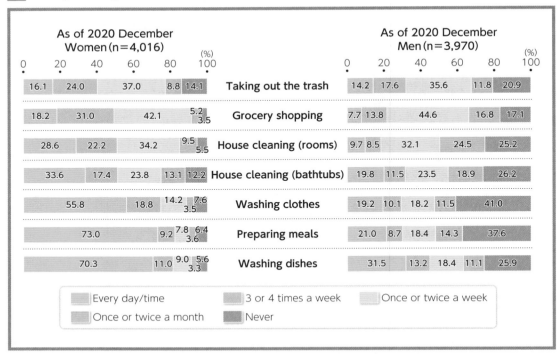

Figure 2. Wife's and Husband's Housework Frequency in December 2020

The white paper on gender equality 2021. Gender Equality Bureau Cabinet Office. より作成
https://www.gender.go.jp/about_danjo/whitepaper/r03/zentai/pdf/r03_tokusyu.pdf

1. Figure 2 shows _____.

2. The source of the bar graph is the _____.

3. The research was conducted in December _____.

4. The graph on the _____ shows how often women did each household task.

5. The graph on the _____ shows the same information for men.

6. The tasks include taking out the trash and grocery shopping.

7. The number of respondents in the survey were _____ women and _____ men.

8. The most frequent task that wives did every time was _____.

9. _____ percent of wives did it almost every time.

10. The task they did least was _____.

11. On the other hand, the most frequent task husbands did every time was _____ at 31.5%, and the task they did least was _____ at less than 8%.

12. The task that most of the husbands never did was _____ at 41% followed by preparing meals at less than _____.

Sharing Your Thoughts

A What do you think?

> **Wives and husbands should do housework equally.**

Your answer:

1. _____
2. _____
3. _____
4. _____
5.

B Express your opinion.

 1-50

Sample conversation

A: Do you think men should do as much housework as women in a household?

B: Absolutely! <u>I have two reasons</u>. <u>First</u>, housework such as cooking, cleaning, and washing are basic things you need to do to live. Imagine you're living alone. You do all the housework, don't you? <u>Second</u>, the number of working couples is increasing. They need to cooperate.

A: You have a point there, but I disagree. Couples need to cooperate, but it doesn't mean that they must do the housework equally. I think each of them can do what they are good at. Don't you think that's more efficient?

B: That may be true, but I think wives will continue to do the hard tasks, such as cooking. I think people will never learn unless they try to do the work.

> **自分の意見を言う時のストラテジー**
>
> 意見を言う時には理由を伝えましょう。複数の理由がある時は、その数を伝え、話す前にディスコースマーカー (First, Second など) を入れると、聞き手が聞きやすくなります。
>
> There are <u>two</u> reasons why I think men should do housework. <u>First</u>, ...<u>Second</u>, ...
>
> **_Exercise_** 私が家で料理をする理由は二つあります。まず、自分の食べたいものを作ることができます。次に、妻が休むことができます。
>
> ....
>
> ....

Group Research

1. Do some research to find the labor participation rates of the countries in the table. Visit the site below which shows labor force participation rates of female and male. Write your findings in the box below. (Labor force participation rate by the World Bank)
   For females, visit https://data.worldbank.org/indicator/SL.TLF.CACT.FE.NE.ZS
   For males, visit https://data.worldbank.org/indicator/SL.TLF.CACT.MA.NE.ZS

	Year	Labor force participation rate, female (% of female participation ages 15+) (National estimate) (A)	Labor force participation rate, male (% of male participation ages 15+) (National estimate) (B)	Ratio of female to male labor force participation (%) (C)=(A)÷(B)	Check the countries which have the largest/ smallest percentage in (A), (B), and (C) e.g. largest (A)/ smallest (A)
Japan					
China					
Russia					
India					
Saudi Arabia					
Sweden					
Poland					
Germany					
Spain					
Egypt					
Nigeria					
U.S.					
Brazil					
Australia					

2. What did you think about the results of your group's research? Talk and write about them in your group.

Preparing for Emergencies

Introduction

CD 1-51

A **Listen to the following news story and fill in the blanks.**

In spring 2021, a **¹**(   ) hotel, HOTEL R9 The Yard Noda, opened in Noda, Chiba Prefecture with **²**(   ) double rooms and 10 **³**(   ) rooms costing from around 8,000 yen to **⁴**(   ) yen per person per night. Its guests visit the area for business or **⁵**(   ). So, why is it unique? The answer is clear to see. The guestrooms are actually wheeled containers occupying a **⁶**(   ) area like cars in a   5 parking lot. The hotel is also called a "**⁷**(   ) hotel." After a **⁸**(   ), these containers can be hitched to tractors and transported **⁹**(   ) to wherever they are needed. For example, some 50 containers were used when a cruise ship at the port of Nagasaki was infected with COVID-19. Medical staff dealing with **¹⁰**(   ) took a rest in them. Goods and services which can be used in various scenarios both   10 in everyday life and emergencies are sometimes called "PhaseFree" goods and services. The widespread use of such goods and services will make us better **¹¹**(   ) for disasters.

B **The following are keywords and phrases from the listening. Look them up in your dictionary and write the meanings.**

1. wheeled containers   _____
2. be hitched to tractors   _____
3. took a rest   _____
4. used in various scenarios   _____
5. both in everyday life and emergencies   _____

C **Talk about these pictures and check your understanding of the listening.**

1.

2.

The double room

3.

a tractor

NOTES

ここの "PhaseFree" という表現は一般社団法人フェーズフリー協会が名付けた和製英語です。一般的な英語表現ではありません。

A What do you think?

What kind of measures can be taken to minimize the damage from natural disasters?

Your answer: _____

•**Passage 1 Title (**)

　　Disaster Prevention Day takes place on September 1st every year. It is a day to commemorate the Great Kanto Earthquake, which occurred on September 1st, 1923. The day has also aroused people's interest in measures for the prevention of disasters. When this day approaches, you can find stores
5 encouraging people to buy emergency goods such as torches and food. Recently goods and services are being produced based on the idea of the "PhaseFree" concept. They are convenient for use both in daily life and in emergencies. For example, the "PhaseFree" furoshiki cloth can be used for wrapping and carrying items but can also be used as a water container in emergencies. "PhaseFree"
10 products help people prepare for disasters even if that is not their main intention.

•**Passage 2 Title (**)

　　Japan is subject to flooding. This is because it has the most sharply dropping rivers in the world. In other words, many rivers flow from high mountains to the sea over very short distances. This means that the rivers can easily flood in downstream areas when there are heavy rains. Moreover, mountains and forests
15 cover more than two-thirds of the land area of Japan, and where people can live accounts for only about 30 percent of the country's surface area. Because of this, many residential areas are situated near mountains and hillsides in the countryside and in lowlands below the level of river water in big cities such as Tokyo and Osaka. When there is heavy rain, such areas are subject to sediment
20 disasters and flooding affecting many people's lives.

•**Passage 3 Title (**)

　　Japan is prone to earthquakes. The most recent massive earthquake that occurred in the country was the Great East Japan Earthquake. It happened along the Japan Trench in 2011 with a magnitude of 9.0. Nearly 16,000 people were killed, and more than 2,500 people are still missing. If another massive
25 earthquake hits along the Japan Trench, particularly late at night in the winter, the tsunami caused by the earthquake could kill nearly 200,000 people. This was an estimate given by the Cabinet Office in December 2021. According to the office, if adequate measures are taken, the number could be reduced by 80%. The measures include building evacuation towers and making residents evacuate
30 quickly.

B Choose a good title for each passage and write the title.

1. The features of residential areas in Japan
2. Why Japan is easily affected by flooding
3. The number of people killed in the event of big earthquakes in Japan
4. Preparations for disasters on September 1st in Japan
5. Why earthquakes occur in Japan   6. Rivers in big cities

C Complete the outline for each passage.

•Passage 1

I. _____

   A. Disaster Prevention Day
      1. Commemorate the _____
      2. Arouse people's interest in _____
   B. Getting emergency goods
      1. Torches and _____
      2. "_____" products

•Passage 2

I. _____

   A. How flooding happens in Japan
      1. Rivers drop sharply over _____ distances
      2. _____ areas of the rivers are affected the most
   B. Residential areas in Japan
      1. Only about _____% of the land area of Japan
      2. Situated near mountains and _____ or _____ the level of river water

•Passage 3

I. _____

   A. The Great East Japan Earthquake
      1. Magnitude of _____
      2. Nearly 16,000 people were _____ and more than 2,500 people are _____
   B. An estimate by the Cabinet Office
      1. The tsunami could kill nearly _____ people
      2. Adequate measures will _____ the number by 80%

D Comprehension questions

1. How can "PhaseFree" products change the way people prepare for disasters?

_____

2. Where are many residential areas situated in big cities in Japan?

_____

3. Give two examples of measures that can reduce the number of people killed in an earthquake.

_____

Key phrases

A Use the following key phrases and translate the Japanese sentences into English.

(例文 1)

The day has also <u>aroused people's interest in</u> measures for the prevention of disasters.

Question

そのニュースは小学校に避難訓練をする興味をわかせた。

- 避難訓練をする：to conduct evacuation drills

Answer

....

(例文 2)

Japan <u>is subject to</u> flooding. / Japan <u>is prone to</u> earthquakes.

Question

その海岸地域は津波の影響を受けやすい。

- 海岸地域：coastal areas

Answer

....

....

(例文 3)

If adequate measures are taken, the number could be <u>reduced by 80%</u>.

Question

その避難訓練は死傷者数を 30 パーセント下げた。

- 避難訓練：evacuation drills ● 死傷者：casualties

Answer

....

Data

 1-55

A Study the figure and the table and fill in the blanks.

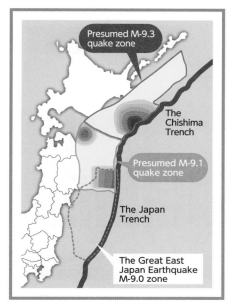

		Summer/daytime	Winter/evening	Winter/midnight
Death caused by the collapse of buildings		About 20 people	About 40 people	About 60 people
Death caused by tsunamis	Early evacuation rate high	About 6,000 people	About 16,000 people	About 47,000 people
	Early evacuation rate low	About 145,000 people	About 162,000 people	About 199,000 people

Table 1. Damage to People in the Case of a Massive Earthquake Along the Japan Trench

Source: The Cabinet Office. 「日本海溝・千島海溝沿いの巨大地震の被害想定について」より作成
https://www.bousai.go.jp/jishin/nihonkaiko_chishima/WG/pdf/21122/shiryo03.pdf

Figure 1. The Presumed Earthquake Zones Along the Chishima Trench and the Japan Trench

Source: The Cabinet Office. 「日本海溝・千島海溝沿いの巨大地震の被害想定について」及び「日本海溝・千島海溝沿いの巨大地震に係る防災対策について」より作成
https://www.bousai.go.jp/jishin/nihonkaiko_chishima/WG/pdf/211221/shiryo05.pdf
https://www.bousai.go.jp/kohou/kouhoubousai/r04/104/news_01.html

Figure 1 shows the areas where big earthquakes in Japan could occur along the two trenches: the 1＿＿＿＿＿ Trench and the 2＿＿＿＿ Trench. A trench is a gap in the ocean bottom where two plates, the layers of the Earth's crust, meet. Earthquakes happen when a plate suddenly moves along the trench. According to the estimate of the National Disaster Management Council, huge earthquakes with 5 magnitudes of 9.1 and 9.3 could affect the coastlines of 3＿＿＿＿ Prefecture, 4＿＿＿＿ Prefecture, and Hokkaido the most.

Table 1 shows the estimated number of 5＿＿＿＿ caused by the collapse of buildings and by 6＿＿＿＿ if a massive earthquake should hit along the Japan Trench. As the numbers show, people who could be killed due to the collapse of 10 buildings are much 7＿＿＿＿ in all the three time periods of day compared to those killed by tsunamis. Furthermore, when the time of the day and the time of the season are compared, tsunamis will affect the lowest number of people when they strike in the 8＿＿＿＿ in 9＿＿＿＿, and the most in the middle of the 10＿＿＿＿ in 11＿＿＿＿. Thus, the worst scenario is when the early 12＿＿＿＿ rate is low in 15 the middle of the night in winter. In this case, it is estimated that about 13＿＿＿＿ people would be killed. However, the number of deaths would be reduced significantly to about 14＿＿＿＿ if people are urged to evacuate quickly and as a result, the early evacuation rate is 15＿＿＿＿.

NOTES

crust: 地殻

B Study the figure and fill in the blanks.

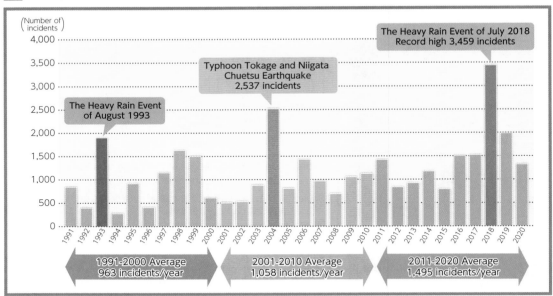

Figure 2. The Number of Sediment Disasters

•Sediment Disasters: 土砂災害　•Number of incidents: 発生件数

Source: The White Paper on Land, Infrastructure, Transport and Tourism, 2021. P46 より作成
https://www.mlit.go.jp/hakusyo/mlit/r02/hakusho/r03/pdf/np102200.pdf

1. The graph shows _____.
2. The source of this graph is _____
    _____.
3. The bars show the number of incidents of _____.
4. As you can see, the year which had the highest number of incidents was _____,
    when _____ incidents of sediment disasters occurred.
5. The heavy _____ in July 2018 contributed to the result.
6. The second highest was in _____ with _____ incidents.
7. A typhoon and an _____ in the Niigata area were responsible for the high
    number.
8. Look at the three horizontal arrows at the bottom.
9. They show the average number of incidents per year in a _____-year period.
10. The average number is increasing every 10 years, from _____ incidents per year
    between 1991 and 2000 to _____ incidents per year between 2011 and 2020.
11. This means that the number has increased nearly _____ times.
12. It can be said that the number of sediment disasters will _____ steadily.

Sharing Your Thoughts

A What do you think?

> **What kind of measures can be taken to minimize the damage from natural disasters?**

Your answer:

1. _____

2. _____

3. _____

4. _____
   _____

5. _____

6. _____

B Express your opinion.   1-57

Sample conversation

A: Tell me your ideas on what kinds of measures we can take to minimize the damage from natural disasters.

B: Well, I think it depends on who takes the measures. If it's individuals, I think first, we need to be prepared for blackouts. We must think about private power generation seriously. On the other hand, if it's the local community such as the local neighborhood association that takes the lead, I think holding evacuation drills will be effective.

A: I see. I think it depends on how much money we're ready to spend on disaster prevention measures. Setting up equipment for private power generation will cost a lot of money. Not everyone can do that, so I think we should start with small things.

B: Can you give me some examples?

> ### 自分の意見を言う時のストラテジー
>
> 条件を分けて、考えを整理しながら話しましょう。
> It depends on…を使って、まずどんな条件で分類できるか伝え、次に、If it is…を使ってそれぞれの
> 条件での考えを分けて説明してみましょう。
>
> It depends on who takes the measures. If it's individuals, …If it's the local community…
>
> *Exercise* それは、災害の起こる時間によります。もし、深夜に起こったなら被害は膨大です。
>
> ....
> ....

1. Do some research to find the latest "PHASE FREE AWARD." Choose a product that received an award. Write your findings in the box below.
   https://aw.phasefree.net/award/

Name of the product	(ASICS RUNWALK)	
Company or organization		
What the product is		
How it can be used in everyday life		
How it can be used in an emergency		
Your evaluation to this product		
Other comments		

2. What did you think about the results of your group's research?
   Talk and write about them in your group.

Ukraine and Afghanistan

Introduction

CD 2-01

A **Listen to the following news story and fill in the blanks.**

Russia launched a military attack on Ukraine on ¹(   )(   ), 2022. The world was shocked as missiles hit buildings, and people were forced into shelters. These events were ²(   ) on TV and shared globally on ³(   ) (   ). Looking back, it seemed that President Vladimir Putin of Russia had a carefully planned strategy. In November, 2021, the U.S. had already reported ⁴(   ) Russian troop movements near the Ukraine border. Although Putin claimed this was part of military ⁵(   ), NATO stationed troops along the border. On February 21, Putin approved ⁶(   ) for two pro-Russian regions in ⁷(   ) Ukraine and sent in troops to support this. Then, on February 24, Russia launched a full-scale attack on Ukraine. By the end of March, more than ⁸(   )(   ) people had fled Ukraine and become ⁹(   ). Putin repeatedly said that the war would not stop until Ukraine was demilitarized to stop the expansion of NATO. He felt that if Ukraine became a NATO member, he would lose control of the ¹⁰(   ) region between Russia and the rest of Europe.

5

10

B **The following are keywords or phrases from the listening. Look them up in your dictionary and write the meanings.**

1. launch a military attack _____
2. be featured _____
3. troops _____
4. flee _____
5. claim _____
6. NATO _____
7. a buffer region _____

C **Talk about these pictures and check your understanding of the listening.**

1.
RUSSIA
■Moscow
■Kyiv
UKRAINE
■ EU member states

2.

3.

A What do you think?

> There are many conflicts in the world. What reasons can you think of?

Your answer: _____

●**Passage 1 Title (   )**

When the Soviet Union was formed by Lenin in 1922, Ukraine became a part of it. But in 1991, when the Soviet Union collapsed, Ukraine gained its independence. Even so, Ukraine continued fighting to secure democracy and its independence through the Orange Revolution in 2004 and the Maidan
5 Revolution in 2014. These conflicts forced Ukraine to choose between being part of Russia or the EU. Thus, Ukraine has been caught between Russia and the rest of Europe for a very long time. Historically and ethnically, Ukraine is strongly connected to Russia. It is also an important region for Russia, both industrially and strategically. The world is hoping Russia's invasion of Ukraine in 2022 will
10 be resolved quickly.

●**Passage 2 Title (   )**

In 2021, the Islamist Taliban took control of Afghanistan after U.S. forces withdrew completely. The stationing of U.S. forces in Afghanistan began after the 9/11 terrorist attacks in 2001. The U.S. government blamed Osama bin Laden, the leader of Al Qaeda, for the 9/11 attacks and suspected the Taliban
15 was protecting him. Because of this, the U.S. attacked Afghanistan, hoping to remove the Taliban from power and destroy Al Qaeda. Despite these efforts, the domestic situation remained unstable. After U.S. forces left, Afghanistan was expected to become a safe haven for terrorists, because of its connections to Al Qaeda.

●**Passage 3 Title (   )**

20 The Taliban is known for its strict belief in traditional Islamic law. In particular, the rights of women and religious minorities are terribly abused. For example, in 2012 Malala Yousafzai was shot and seriously injured for exercising her right to go to school. Other severe punishments include cutting off people's hands and public execution. Although the Taliban returned to power in 2021,
25 they killed more than 100 officials, journalists, police, and politicians. Additionally, with the struggling economy, it was estimated that around 23 million people (half the population) faced severe hunger, and about nine million of them were on the brink of starvation in the winter of 2021. Desperate families were forced to do unimaginable things like sell their children and arrange
30 marriages for very young girls.

B Choose a good title for each passage from the choices below.

1. Human rights for women
2. The current situation in Afghanistan
3. The Taliban and terrorists in Afghanistan
4. The modern history of Ukraine
5. Ukraine: Caught between Europe and Russia
6. A safe haven for terrorists

C Fill in the blanks and write an outline for each passage.

•Passage 1

I. _____

    A. When the Soviet Union was formed by Lenin in _____, Ukraine became a part of it.

    B. When the Soviet Union collapsed in 1991, Ukraine gained its _____.

    C. Ukraine continued fighting to secure democracy and its independence.

        1. the _____ Revolution in 2004

        2. the _____ Revolution in 2014

•Passage 2

I. _____

    A. In 2021, the Taliban took control of Afghanistan.

        1. U.S. _____ withdrew completely from Afghanistan.

        2. The stationing of U.S. troops began because of the 9/11 _____ in 2001.

        3. The U.S. government attacked the Taliban and _____.

        4. After U.S. forces left, it was expected that Afghanistan would become _____ for terrorists.

•Passage 3

I. _____

    A. The Taliban is known for its strict belief in traditional Islamic law.

        1. The rights of _____ and religious _____ are terribly abused.

        2. Other severe punishments include _____ people's hands.

        3. The Taliban killed more than _____ former officials, police, and politicians.

    B. The economy was struggling.

    C. Around 23 million people faced _____ in 2021.

D Comprehension questions

1. What is Ukraine caught between?

_____

2. What was the main concern after U.S. forces left Afghanistan?

_____

3. What is the Taliban known for?

_____

Key phrases

A Use the following key phrases and translate the Japanese sentences into English.

例文 1

~ , Ukraine <u>has been caught</u> between Russia and the rest of Europe ~ .

Question

このEU関連の問題で、イギリスは2つのグループの意見に挟まれていた。

Answer

....

例文 2

~ , Afghanistan was expected to <u>become a safe haven</u> for terrorists, ~

Question

いくつかのアフリカの国が過激派の安全地帯になりつつある。

Answer

....

例文 3

The Taliban <u>is known for</u> its strict belief in traditional Islamic law.

Question

イスラム国は捕虜の非人道的な扱いが有名である。

• 非人道的な扱い：inhumane treatment

Answer

....

Data

 2-05

A Study the figure and fill in the blanks.

Source: Institute for the Study of War (as of 23:00 GMT, 1 March)

Figure 1. How Much of Ukraine Does Russia Control?

Source: Institute for the Study of War (as of 23:00 GMT, 1 March) より作成

This map of Ukraine shows how much of the country Russia controlled as of
1_____, 2022. The source of this map is 2_____
_____. The red areas were under 3_____ control. Crimea is
red but also surrounded by a black line. This means that Crimea was annexed by
Russia in 4_____. At that time, there was an incident similar to what happened in ⁵
Luhansk and 5_____ in February 2022. Many pro-Russian people lived in these
two areas and pushed for their freedom from Ukraine. Putin supported them when they
declared their 6_____ and launched an attack on Ukraine. Kyiv is the
7_____ of Ukraine, and fierce battles continued near the area. So, many people
tried to go to Lviv although it is the country's westernmost city, and about 8_____ ¹⁰
km away. It is one of the gateways to Europe because it is near 9_____.

B Study the figure and fill in the blanks.

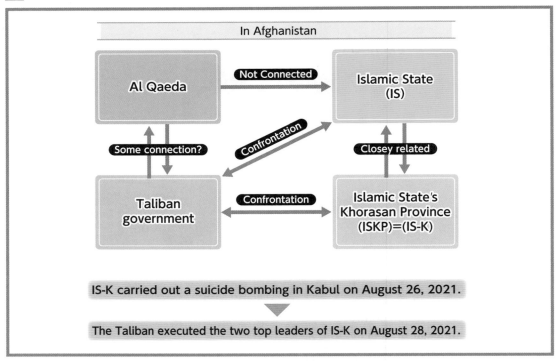

Figure 2. Terrorism Can Be Caused by Conflicts Among Islamic Extremists

Nihonkeizai Newspaper: August 27, 2021 より作成
https://www.nikkei.com/article/DGXZQOGM274BJ0X20C21A8000000/
A diagram was translated from Japanese to English by the author

1. Figure 2 is a diagram which shows the relationship among Islamist extremists as of August _____.

2. It indicates that terrorism can be caused by _____ among Islamic extremists.

3. There seems to be some connection between the Taliban and _____, but Al Qaeda and the Islamic State (IS) are not _____.

4. IS confronted the Taliban, but IS and IS-Khorasan Province (IS-K) are _____ _____. This means that the Taliban is also against IS-K. IS-K is considered to be the most brutal terrorist group.

5. In fact, on _____ in 2021, while the Taliban tried to create a new government, IS-K carried out a _____ in Kabul and killed more Taliban members than American soldiers.

6. As a result of this incident, the Taliban and U.S. forces killed the two top leaders of _____ on August 28.

7. Judging from these actions, it seems it will take time for the Taliban to function as a _____.

Sharing Your Thoughts

A What do you think?

> **There are many conflicts in the world. What reasons can you think of?**

Your answer:

1. _____

2. _____

3. _____

4. _____

5. _____

6. _____

B Express your opinion.

 2-07

Sample conversation

A: Even in the modern world, a strong desire for power and a threat to security can be responsible for starting a conflict, as in the past.

B: Yeah, the reasons for starting a war might not have changed so much.

A: That's because the nature of people does not change.

B: But in this conflict, both leaders are taking advantage of advances in technology.

A: That's true. Both leaders use and control social media a lot.

B: Yes, in particular, both of them made speeches and used them to appeal to the world many times.

A: For us, <u>the bottom line is</u> that we shouldn't be fooled by false information and increase our hatred.

B: You can say that again. And, <u>the most important thing is</u> figuring out how to stop this war through some sort of compromise.

┌─ 自分の意見を言う時のストラテジー ─┐

肝心なことは〜、大事なことは〜という表現で重要性を強調します。

<u>The bottom line is</u> that we shouldn't be fooled.

<u>The most important thing is</u> figuring out how to stop this war through some sort of compromise.

Exercise 肝心なことは、強国の暴挙を支持しないことです。

....

1. Do some research to find various reasons of conflicts. Write your findings in the box below.

Conflict areas	Who fought against who?	Reasons and results
1.		
2.		
3.		
4.		

2. What did you think about the results of your group's research? Talk and write about them in your group.

Digital Society

Introduction

🔊 2-08

A Listen to the following news story and fill in the blanks.

In January 2022, the Panasonic Group announced it would make a ¹( ) entry into a metaverse-related device, namely virtual goggles for ²( ) in a three-dimensional (3D) virtual space. This virtual space is often called the metaverse, which includes business meetings, workshops, lectures, ³( ) ( ), live concerts, and PC games. Participants send avatars into these spaces to ₅ communicate with other avatars. Meta (previously Facebook), Nike, Microsoft, Disney, Sony, GREE, and various ⁴( ) are planning to expand into this new market. Mark Zuckerberg, Meta's CEO, expects the number of participants in online events to reach 1 billion within the next 10 years. Many consider this ⁵( ) new market to be a direct result of the COVID-19 pandemic, which limited people's ₁₀ ⁶( ) of activity and increased demand for ⁷( ) types of services. While the metaverse can make life productive and convenient, there is concern about its ⁸( ) effect on mental health. Our hearing and ⁹( ) might also be ¹⁰( ) if we spend too much time in a virtual space.

B The following are keywords or phrases from the listening. Look them up in your dictionary and write the meanings.

1. make a full-scale entry into _____
2. metaverse-related device _____
3. three-dimensional virtual space _____
4. workshops _____
5. avatars _____
6. start-ups _____
7. non-contact types of services _____

C Talk about these pictures and check your understanding of the listening.

1.
VR Space

2.

3.

←	COVID-19
→	Mental health Hearing & vision

Reading

A What do you think?

> Digital Society has a light side and a dark side. When it comes to the dark side, what kinds of things can you think of?

Your answer: _____

• **Passage 1 Title (   )**

Modern society is digital-centric, meaning that most people depend on Internet technology to research, access, and provide information. As a result, the Big Four tech companies, collectively known as GAFA, have emerged as dominant organizations. GAFA is an acronym for Google, Apple, Facebook, and Amazon. Because of their huge market share and massive ownership of consumer data, they are often criticized for being monopolistic and suppressing competition. Meanwhile, the next companies driving the newest trend, called MT SaaS, are rapidly expanding by providing cloud services. The companies that make up this group are Microsoft, Twilio, Shopify, Amazon, Adobe, and Salesforce.

• **Passage 2 Title (   )**

Internet shutdown is used by a growing number of governments, especially in Asian and African countries. When governments want to limit dissatisfaction, or they find anti-government information on social media, they block Internet access. In January 2022, authorities took this action in Kazakhstan when unrest and violence spread. Internet access was blocked in November 2020 in Ethiopia. In Myanmar, it was completely shut down after a military coup in February 2021. Internet shutdown has become a powerful tool to stop political protests against the government. Unfortunately, it also violates the digital freedom of common people.

• **Passage 3 Title (   )**

Personal and classified information is at risk. Recently, it was discovered that Zoom's Wi-Fi passwords had been detected on a server in Beijing in 2020. The Global Security Research Center of Toronto University warned that any politicians, industries, and medical facilities with highly confidential information should not use Zoom as a communication tool. In 2022, the Japanese government decided to use only Japanese companies such as NTT, Fujitsu, or NEC to handle classified information. In Japan, about 80% of personal information leakage happened during a cyberattack against listed companies on a stock exchange market in 2021. If it continues to happen, information leakage will eventually lead to serious security issues for Japan.

B Choose a good title for each passage from the choices below.
1. Internet shutdown by governments
2. Giant companies
3. GAFA's huge power
4. Information leakage
5. Countries in Asia and Africa
6. Personal and classified information

C Fill in the blanks and write an outline for each passage.
•Passage 1
I. _____
   A. Modern society is digital-centric.
   B. The Big Four tech companies, known as _____, have emerged.
      1. It is an acronym for _____, Apple, Facebook, and Amazon.
      2. They are criticized for being _____ and suppressing competition.
   C. The next companies driving the newest trend called _____ are expanding.

•Passage 2
I. _____
   A. Purposes
      1. to limit dissatisfaction
      2. to find _____ information on _____
   B. Examples
      1. In Kazakhstan in 2022
      2. In _____ in 2020
      3. In Myanmar in 2021

•Passage 3
I. _____
   A. Examples
      1. In 2020, it was discovered that _____ Wi-Fi passwords passed through a server in _____.
      2. In 2022, the Japanese government decided to use only Japanese companies to handle _____ information.
      3. In Japan, about ____% of personal information leakage happened during a _____ against listed companies on a stock exchange market.

D Comprehension questions
1. What is the problem of GAFA?
_____
2. Why did the Myanmar government block Internet access?
_____
3. What kinds of people should avoid using Zoom?
_____

Key phrases

A Use the following key phrases and translate the Japanese sentences into English.

例文 1

Modern society is digital-centric, <u>meaning that</u> most people depend on Internet technology to research, access, and provide information.

Question

日本は、超高齢化社会になった。それはつまり、私たちは近い将来、労働力不足に直面することを意味している。

• 超高齢化：a super-aged society

Answer

....

....

例文 2

〜, authorities <u>took this action</u> in Kazakhstan when unrest and violence spread.

•take an action：ある行動をとる（いろいろな選択肢がある）•take action：行動を起こす

Question

政府は反政府的な動きに、インターネットを遮断するという行動をとった。

Answer

....

....

例文 3

Information leakage will eventually <u>lead to</u> serious security issues for Japan.

Question

個人情報漏れは、詐欺などの犯罪につながる恐れがある。

• 詐欺：fraud

Answer

....

86

Data

A Study the figure and fill in the blanks.

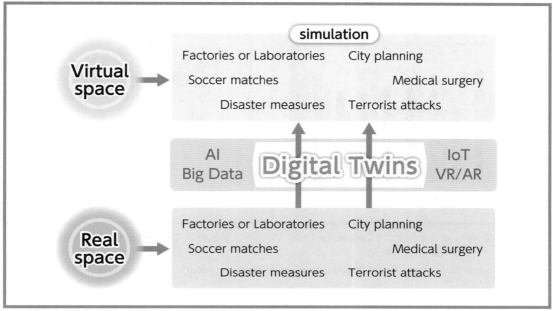

Figure 1. Digital Twins

Source: SoftBank Created by the author, Based on the diagram
https://cdn-ak.f.st-hatena.com/images/fotolife/a/aq-sb-01/20200917/20200917164055.png

There is another technology related to VR called "Digital Twins" as shown in Figure 1. The source of this diagram is $_1$_____. Digital Twins is technology that reproduces $_2$_____ space in a virtual space by using big data collected by IoT. It creates an environment in virtual space that is identical to a physical one, much like the reflection of a mirror. That's why the term "twins" is used. Digital Twins use $_3$_____, big data, IoT, and $_4$_____. 5

This technology has been applied in factories or $_5$_____, city planning, $_6$_____, medical surgery, $_7$_____ measures, and $_8$_____ attacks. In the virtual space, it is possible to see how people, machines, or materials move or react under certain conditions. In other words, $_9$_____ is possible 10 without any real risk or damage. In short, people can use trial and error before a product is made, a real game begins, or a disaster happens.

NOTES

AR (augmented reality: 拡張現実) 実際には存在しないが、ゴーグルをかけると実際のシーンの中にないものが浮かぶ。

B Study the figures and fill in the blanks.

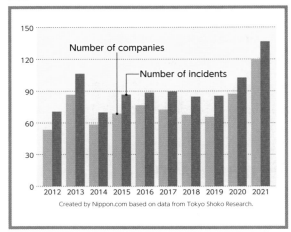

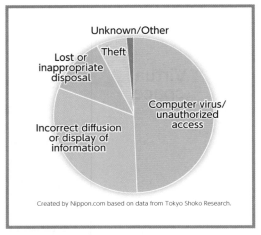

Figure 2. Annual Incidents of Leaked or Lost Personal Information

Figure 3. Causes of Leaked and Lost Information

Source: Nippon.com "Over 5 Million Individuals' Information Leaked or Lost in Japan in 2021" Feb 9, 2022
https://www.nippon.com/en/japan-data/h01241/

Figure 2

1. Figure 2 shows the number of annual incidents of _____
   _____.

2. The source of this bar graph is _____.

3. The blue bar shows the number of _____, and the light blue bar shows the number of _____.

4. The horizontal axis shows the years from _____ to 2021.

5. The vertical axis shows the number of _____ and _____.

6. In 2012, the number of incidents was about 70, but in 2021, it was about 140, so it _____ in 10 years.

7. In 2021, the number of incidents and companies was _____, involving information on over 5 million individuals.

Figure 3

8. Figure 3 shows the breakdown of _____ of leaked or lost information for about 140 incidents.

9. Computer viruses and unauthorized access accounted for _____ of these incidents.

10. It can be said that computer viruses and unauthorized access are two of the major causes of _____ and _____ information.

Sharing Your Thoughts

A What do you think?

> Digital Society has a light side and a dark side. When it comes to the dark side, what kinds of things can you think of?

Your answer:

1. _____

2. _____

3. _____

4. _____

5. _____

B Express your opinion.

 2-14

Sample conversation

A: Our society has become digital more quickly than I expected.

B: I feel the same way, but it's exciting, isn't it? The metaverse might provide a wide variety of opportunities for us to participate in business meetings, workshops, or even social gatherings while we're at home. We can be released from the limits of space and time.

A: That's an amazing point of the metaverse, but I have concerns. People might create several avatars and use them in a different VR, but their characters and behavior might not be true. Furthermore, even if we make friends with other avatars, we can't fully trust the relationship.

B: That's true and might be a problem. Furthermore, if we have trouble with other avatars, it might be confusing because there are no rules or laws in the metaverse.

> **自分の意見を言う時のストラテジー**
>
> 反対の意見を言う時は I disagree だけではなく、他のフレーズも知っておくと良いです。
>
> I have a great concern about it. / I have a little doubt about it.
> I'm concerned about ～
>
> *Exercise* 私は他のアバターとの友人関係が心配です。

1. Do some research to find various services by avatars. Write your findings in the box below.

	Companies	Services by avatars
1		
2		
3		
4		
5		
6		
7		

2. What did you think about the results of your group's research? Talk and write about them in your group.

Climate and Infectious Diseases

Introduction

2-15

A **Listen to the following news story and fill in the blanks.**

In August 2014, Japan was tackling its first ¹( ) of a tropical disease in almost 70 years. An outbreak of dengue fever was last recorded in Japan in ²( ), according to the Ministry of Health, Labor and Welfare. The following month, the Tokyo Metropolitan Government ³( ) certain areas of Yoyogi Park due to the discovery of ⁴( ) carrying the dengue virus. The discovery confirmed the 5 park as the site of ⁵( ) for dozens of people. Not long before, all of the patients had spent time in or near the park. Japan sees ⁶( ) cases of dengue fever each year, mostly from tourists who catch it while traveling to ⁷( ) regions. Domestic mosquitoes could have also picked up the dengue virus from ⁸( ) and passed it on. Patients are struck with high ⁹( ) and severe 10 joint pain. Most cases involve mild ¹⁰( ), but severe cases may require hospital treatment.

B **The following are keywords or phrases from the listening. Look them up in your dictionary and write the meanings.**

1. outbreak _____
2. tropical _____
3. dengue fever _____
4. mosquito _____
5. virus _____
6. infection _____
7. symptom _____

C **Talk about these pictures and check your understanding of the listening.**

1.
2.
3.

A What do you think?

How can we prevent the spread of tropical diseases in Japan?

Your answer: _____

•Passage 1 **Title (   )**

Singapore is situated near the equator and has a tropical climate, with abundant rainfall, high temperatures, and high humidity all year round. Many of its climate variables do not show large month-to-month variation. Singapore's climate is characterized by two monsoon seasons. The Northeast Monsoon
5 occurs from December to early March, and the Southwest Monsoon from June to September. The strong wind brings about heavy rainfall. Higher rainfall occurs from November to January, when the major tropical rain belt is positioned near the country. The driest month is February, when the rain belt has moved south.

•Passage 2 **Title (   )**

10 Dengue fever is an illness transmitted by the bite of a mosquito. A person infected with the virus experiences a fever accompanied by headaches along with muscle and joint pain. Severe infections can result in death but they are less than one percent of the cases. Climate change has affected the spread of dengue. Warmer temperatures result in higher transmission due to the accelerated
15 development of the mosquito and shorter incubation period of the virus. The most effective way to control the mosquito population is to prevent breeding. Mosquitoes breed in standing water, so in Singapore, if households leave water containers uncovered, they are fined at least S$200. When you enter areas where there are mosquitoes, you should apply insect repellent.

•Passage 3 **Title (   )**

20 Weather is a major motivator for mosquito activity. Mosquitoes are insects and so are cold-blooded. This means that their body temperature is more or less the same as their environment, since they don't have the ability to regulate their internal temperatures. Rainfall creates ideal breeding conditions for mosquitoes because they lay eggs in standing water. More rain means greater potential for
25 mosquito breeding. Mosquitoes love warm climates. They are active once temperatures are consistently above 10 degrees Celsius, but activity tends to jump when the temperature reaches 26 degrees and above. Warmer temperatures make mosquitoes hungrier for blood meals. In winter, mosquitoes disappear. Since they are cold-blooded, they hibernate when temperatures fall below 10
30 degrees.

B **Choose a good title for each passage from the choices below.**

1. Dengue fever

2. Climate change in Singapore

3. Cold-blooded insects

4. Climate of Singapore

5. Mosquito activity

6. Two monsoon seasons

C **Fill in the blanks and write an outline for each passage.**

•Passage 1

I. _____

   A. Location

      1. near the_____

   B. Climate

      1. _____ climate

      2. abundant _____

      3. high _____ and high _____

•Passage 2

I. _____

   A. Transmission

      1. the bite of a _____

   B. Spread

      1. _____ temperatures result in higher transmission

   C. Measures

      1. prevent _____ of mosquitoes

•Passage 3

I. _____

   A. Rainfall

      1. ideal _____ conditions

   B. Warm climates

      1. active when temperatures are _____

      2. activity tends to jump when it is _____

D **Comprehension questions**

1. What are the characteristics of Singapore's climate?

_____

2. How is dengue fever transmitted?

_____

3. What are ideal breeding conditions for mosquitoes?

_____

Key phrases

A Use the following key phrases and translate the Japanese sentences into English.

例文 1

Singapore <u>is situated</u> near the equator.

Question

日本は東アジアに位置している。

Answer

例文 2

A person <u>infected with</u> the virus experiences a fever.

Question

その兵士はマラリアに感染した。

- マラリア：malaria

Answer

例文 3

Activity <u>tends to</u> jump when the temperature reaches 26 degrees and above.

Question

日本人は長時間働く傾向がある。

- 長時間：long hours

Answer

Data

 2-19

A Study the figure and table and fill in the blanks.

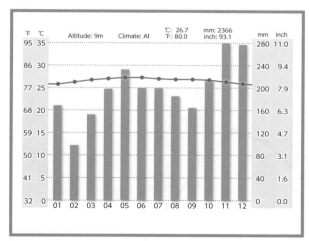

Figure 1. Climate Graph of Singapore

Source: Climate-Data.org "Climate: Singapore" より作成
https://en.climate-data.org/asia/singapore-107/

1st	2nd	3rd
A(Tropical)	f(Rainforest)	
	m(Monsoon)	
	w(Savanna, Wet)	
	s(Savanna, Dry)	
B(Arid)	w(Desert)	
	s(Steppe)	
		h(Hot)
		k(Cold)
		n(With frequent fog)
C(Temperate)	s(Dry summer)	
	w(Dry winter)	
	f(Without dry season)	
		a(Hot summer)
		b(Warm summer)
		c(Cold summer)
D(Cold[continental])	s(Dry summer)	
	w(Dry winter)	
	f(Without dry season)	
		a(Hot summer)
		b(Warm summer)
		c(Cold summer)
		d(Very cold winter)
E(Polar)	T(Tundra)	
	F(Eternal winter[ice cap])	

Table 1. Köppen Climate Classification Scheme Symbols Description Table

Source: Köppen climate classification "Köppen climate classification scheme symbols description table" より作成
https://en.wikipedia.org/wiki/K%C3%B6ppen_climate_classification

Figure 1 is a 1_____ graph for Singapore. A climate graph is a time-based graphic representation of a location's average 2_____ and 3_____. It is used to compare the climate in different places. The red 4_____ graph shows average temperature and the blue 5_____ graph shows average precipitation. The horizontal line shows 6_____ of the year and the 7_____ line shows average temperature and precipitation.

According to Köppen climate classification, the climate in Singapore is described as Af. The first letter is "A" and the second letter is "f," which means 8_____ rainforest climate. The temperature averages 9_____°C. The average temperatures are always above 10_____°C all year round. With an average of 27.4°C, May is the warmest month. January has the lowest average temperature of the year at 25.8°C.

Singapore has a significant amount of precipitation during the year. The precipitation is around 2,366 mm per year. The driest month is 11_____, when there is 97 mm of precipitation. With an average of 280 mm, the most precipitation occurs in 12_____.

5

10

15

Data

B Study the figure and fill in the blanks.

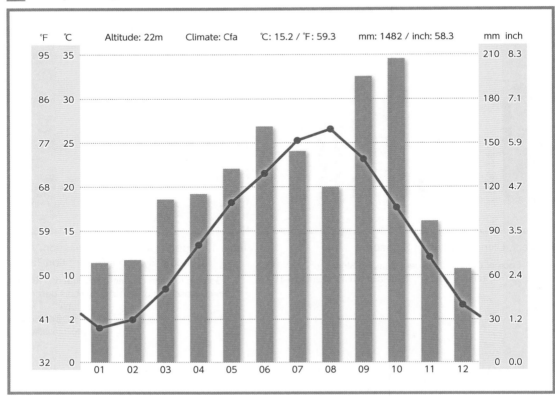

Figure 2. Climate Graph for Tokyo

Source: Climate-Data.org "Climate: Tokyo" より作成
https://en.climate-data.org/asia/japan/tokyo-2442/

1. Figure 2 is _____.
2. The climate in Tokyo is classified as _____.
   It is a _____ climate without a _____ season and it is hot in summer.
3. The temperature averages _____°C.
4. In a year, the rainfall is _____ mm.
5. The average temperatures vary depending on the _____.
6. The average temperature is above _____°C in July and August.
7. The average temperature is below _____°C from December to March.
8. _____ falls throughout the year in Tokyo.
9. The months with abundant rainfall in Tokyo are _____, _____, and _____.

Sharing Your Thoughts

A What do you think?

How can we prevent the spread of tropical diseases in Japan?

Your answer:

1. _____

2. _____

3. _____

4. _____

5. _____

B Express your opinion.

 2-21

Sample conversation

A: I think we can prevent the spread of dengue fever in Japan by protecting ourselves from mosquitoes.

B: How can we do that?

A: For example, we should wear clothes with long sleeves or use insect repellent when we go to forests or parks. Also, people arriving from abroad should be checked carefully at the airport.

B: I think these measures are effective, but we need to think about how climate change can affect the spread of the tropical diseases in Japan. I learned that mosquitoes love warm climates and they are very active when the temperature is 26 degrees and above. This means a greater chance of infection. For this reason, we should make efforts to stop global warming.

> **自分の意見を言う時のストラテジー**
>
> 具体例を挙げることにより、相手と具体的な方策を共有することができます。
>
> For example, we should wear clothes with long sleeves.
>
> **Exercise** 例えば、水の入った容器を外に放置しないことが大切です。
>
> ....

Group Research

1. Do some research to find how climate change will affect the occurrence of the following infectious diseases.

Diseases	Mode of transmission	Effects of climate change
Dengue fever (デング熱)		
Malaria (マラリア)		
Cholera (コレラ)		
Japanese encephalitis (日本脳炎)		

2. What did you think about the results of your group's research? Talk and write about them in your group.

Overtourism and Undertourism

Introduction

🔊 2-22

A **Listen to the following news story and fill in the blanks.**

Globally, the number of people traveling by ¹( ) increased steadily until the outbreak of the COVID-19 pandemic. The number is expected to ²( ) again once the pandemic is over. According to the Air Transport Action Group, aviation was responsible for ³( ) of CO_2 emissions from all transport sources in 2020. Therefore, zero-emission technologies are being developed. Airbus, the world's leading aircraft ⁴( ), announced in 2022 that it plans to develop the world's first zero-emission commercial airplanes by ⁵( ). The planes will carry hydrogen ⁶( ) as fuel instead of oil. This means that ⁷( ) hydrogen will be burned with oxygen in a gas turbine, so there will be no CO_2 ⁸( ) released into the atmosphere. The designs of the new aircraft come in three types. One of them has a "blended-wing" body. Unlike the conventional "tube-and-wing" aircraft, the wings create ⁹( ) interior spaces for passengers and storage of hydrogen tanks. Moreover, they use less ¹⁰( ) and produce less ¹¹( ). The future of aviation might change drastically by developing planes that are ¹²( ).

5

10

B **The following are keywords or phrases from the listening. Look them up in your dictionary and write the meanings.**

1. aviation _____
2. zero-emission _____
3. the world's leading aircraft manufacturer _____
4. hydrogen _____
5. released into the atmosphere _____
6. a "blended-wing" body _____
7. the conventional "tube-and-wing" aircraft _____

C **Talk about these pictures and check your understanding of the listening.**

1.

2.

Hydrogen tanks

3.

"Blended-wing" body

A What do you think?

> How can people enjoy traveling without damaging the environment and the quality of life (QOL) of the local people?

Your answer: _____

•Passage 1 **Title (**)

It is estimated that by 2030, the number of tourists traveling globally will surpass three billion. The number has increased steadily since the 1960s, when jumbo jets were launched. Travel expenses and time were greatly reduced and made overseas travel affordable. Later, the emergence of low-cost carriers 5 expanded tourist inflows even more. The Internet has also accelerated the number of travelers. It made it easy for people to book flights and hotels. Moreover, Airbnb has also made overseas travel popular by offering reasonably priced accommodations and adding more capacity. However, the rise in tourist inflows has caused overtourism, or a state of overcapacity, in certain destinations. 10 In Japan, they are Kyoto, Kamakura, and Niseko, to name just a few.

•Passage 2 **Title (**)

Overtourism refers to a situation where the inflow of tourists exceeds the capacity of the local area. Cities such as Amsterdam, Barcelona, and Venice, suffer from overtourism. The places are crowded, and traffic congestion frequently occurs. Anti-social behavior by tourists, such as littering and making 15 noise, are also observed. Excessive visitors also cause environmental problems such as increasing CO_2 emissions and water consumption, and damage to nature and heritage sites. These phenomena decrease the quality of life of residents, too. In 2021, Amsterdam issued an ordinance limiting the number of tourists to 20 million overnight stays per year. If the number exceeds this, the city will take 20 measures such as increasing tourist tax or limiting Airbnb availability and alcohol sales in certain areas.

•Passage 3 **Title (**)

The COVID-19 pandemic led to "undertourism" or no tourism at all. This had a great impact on all sectors of the tourism industry, such as hotels, souvenir shops, museums, transportation services, and travel agencies. Some people lost 25 their jobs, and some had to close down their businesses. Amsterdam is known to be the first city to issue an ordinance to tackle overtourism, but it also set a minimum limit for tourists in its regulation. If the number of overnight stays per year falls below 10 million, the local government will intervene to promote tourism. This means that the local people and the government admit that there 30 should be a good balance in the number of tourists to sustain the local economy.

B **Choose a good title for each passage from the choices below.**

1. The negative effects of excessive visitors
2. The emergence of low-cost carriers
3. How tourism became popular around the world
4. Sustaining the tourism-related economy
5. The issue of a decreasing number of residents
6. How to behave at tourist sites around the world

C **Fill in the blanks and write an outline for each passage.**

•Passage 1

I. _____

    A. What made tourism popular

        1. The emergence of jumbo jets, _____, the Internet, and

        _____

    B. The result of tourist inflows

•Passage 2

I. _____

    A. The negative effects

        1. Traffic congestion

        2. Tourists' _____

        3. _____ problems

        4. Decrease in the quality of life of residents

    B. An _____ issued in Amsterdam

        1. Limit to the number of _____

•Passage 3

I. _____

    A. The decline of tourism

        1. Affects everyone working in the _____ industry

    B. A good balance needed to sustain the local economy

        1. Amsterdam's ordinance to keep a good _____ in the number of tourists

D **Comprehension questions**

1. How did Airbnb make tourism more popular?

_____

2. What did the city of Amsterdam do to tackle overtourism problems?

_____

3. What do the local people and the government of Amsterdam admit?

_____

Key phrases

A Use the following key phrases and translate the Japanese sentences into English.

例文 1

In Japan, they are Kyoto, Kamakura, and Niseko, <u>to name just a few</u>.

Question

植物を踏み荒らしたり、花を摘んだりすることは、自然遺産での観光客の悪い振る舞いのほんの数例である。

- 踏み荒らす：trample on　　• 自然遺産：natural heritage sites

Answer

....
....

例文 2

If the number exceeds this, the city will <u>take measures</u>.

Question

その市は観光客の数を減らすために何か対策を取る必要がある。

Answer

....

例文 3

This <u>had a great impact on</u> all sectors of the tourism industry.

Question

新型コロナウイルス感染症の流行は、観光産業に大きな影響を与えた。

Answer

....

Data

2-26

A Study the figure and fill in the blanks.

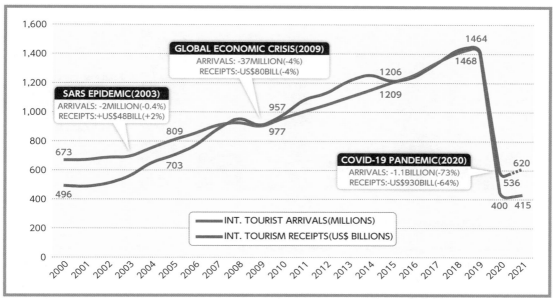

Figure 1. International Tourist Arrivals and Tourism Receipts 2000-2021

Source: UNWTO WORLD TOURISM BAROMETER JANUARY 2022. UNWTO. "© UNWTO, 92844/15/22"
https://webunwto.s3.eu-west-1.amazonaws.com/s3fs-public/2022-01/220118-Barometersmall.pdf?_PBIQdr4u_
qM0w56.l0NpfGPzylGu6Md

    Figure 1 shows international tourist $_1$_____ and tourism $_2$_____. The blue line indicates the change in the arrival $_3$_____ of international tourists in millions between 2000 and 2021. The red line indicates how much $_4$_____ was received by them in billions of dollars during the same period. The source of the data is the United Nations World Tourism Organization (UNWTO).

    As the lines show, both the number of international arrivals and tourism receipts grew steadily from 2000 to $_5$_____. The growth decreased slightly in $_6$_____ and $_7$_____ due to the SARS epidemic and the global economic crisis, respectively, but recovered soon. However, in 2020 when the $_8$_____ hit the world, the number of international arrivals and the money received from them $_9$_____ suddenly. The annual number of international arrivals $_{10}$_____ by 73% from nearly 1.5 billion to 400 million. Meanwhile, the annual tourism receipts also fell by $_{11}$_____% from nearly $_{12}$_____ trillion dollars to 536 billion dollars. Although both numbers increased just a little in 2021, it seems that it will take several years before the number of international tourists and the related economy fully recover to the pre-pandemic level.

B Study the figure and fill in the blanks.

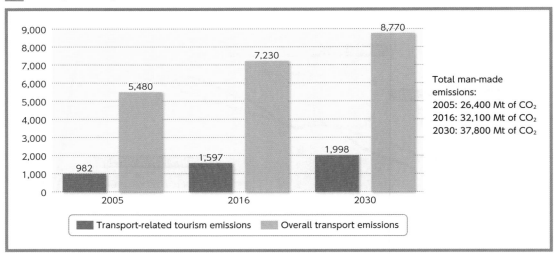

Figure 2. Overall Transport Emissions and Transport-related Emissions from Tourism, 2005, 2016 and 2030(Mt of CO₂)

Source: "Transport related CO₂ emissions of the tourism sector – modelling results". (2019). World Tourism Organization (UNWTO) and International Transport Forum (ITF). より作成 "© UNWTO, 92844/15/22" https://www.e-unwto.org/doi/epdf/10.18111/9789284416660

1. Figure 2 shows overall transport emissions and transport-related emissions from _____ in 2005, 2016, and 2030.

2. The dark blue bars show the amount of transport-related tourism emissions in _____ (Mt), while the light blue bars show that of _____ transport emissions.

3. The description on the right shows the amount of total _____ CO₂ emissions.

4. The result for 2030 in the graph shows the estimation made by this report, which was issued by the _____ (UNWTO) and the International Transport Forum (ITF).

5. In 2005, transport-related tourism emissions accounted for _____ million tons.

6. This amount was about _____% of the overall transport emissions and 3.7% of the total man-made emissions.

7. In 2030 the tourism emissions were estimated to increase to _____ million tons.

8. This amount was nearly _____% of the overall transport emissions and 5.3% of the total man-made emissions.

9. It can be said that the amount of CO₂ emissions from tourism will _____ its share of the total transport and man-made CO₂ emissions.

Sharing Your Thoughts

A What do you think?

> **How can people enjoy traveling without damaging the environment and the quality of life (QOL) of the local people?**

Your answer:

1. _____

2. _____

3. _____

4. _____

5. _____

B Express your opinion.

 2-28

Sample conversation

A: Traveling is exciting but overtourism is a problem now. How do you think we can realize sustainable tourism?

B: Well, for me, sustainable tourism means a win-win relationship between tourists and the local people. So, I think I would choose Ecobnb, when I book a vacation.

A: Ecobnb? What's that? I've never heard of it.

B: It's a platform that offers you eco-friendly travel. For example, it introduces you to less touristy places and hotels where local organic products and clean energy are used.

A: That's a good idea. I would choose car-free tourism. I would leave my car and use public transportation. <u>At least</u>, this would ease traffic congestion and reduce CO_2 emissions.

【 自分の意見を言う時のストラテジー 】

意見を言う時に、すべての条件に合致する意見を見つけ出すことは難しいものです。「少なくともこのポイントにおいては効果があるのではないか」、と言いたい時に、**At least…** を使うことができます。限られた条件のもとでも、お互いに意見を出し合うことで大きな解決策が見つかるかもしれません。

    <u>At least</u>, this would ease traffic congestion and reduce CO_2 emissions.

Exercise ホテルが節水機能付き蛇口を使えば、少なくともその地域の水の消費量は削減されるでしょう。

• 節水機能付き蛇口：water flow reducer taps

....

....

1. Do some research to find some of the places that have faced overtourism. Check the actions taken there. Write your findings in the box below.

Places	Example of damages/ inconvenience	Who took the action	How
(Amsterdam)			
(Kyoto)			
(Mt. Fuji)			

2. What did you think about the results of your group's research? Talk and write about them in your group.

UNIT 13

Multicultural Exchange in Japan

Introduction

🎵 2-29

A **Listen to the following news story and fill in the blanks.**

On April 7, 2022, a sister and a brother from Ukraine ¹( ) in the opening
ceremony of a public ²( ) school in Japan. They had come to Aichi
Prefecture to escape the war in their country. The sister was ³( ) years old, and
her brother was 9. Their lessons included studying English and ⁴( )
education with Japanese classmates and taking Japanese language lessons. They also ⁵
received tablet computers to ⁵( ) lessons into Ukrainian. According to
Japan's Ministry of Education, the total number of elementary to high-school students
from other countries in 2019 was more than ⁶( ). In 2021, it was found that
⁷( ) of these students needed special instruction in Japanese, and 47,627
were of foreign nationality. Of these 47,627, 25.1% spoke ⁸( ), 20.9% ₁₀
Chinese, and 15.7% Tagalog. About ⁹( )% of foreign students received
instruction in Japanese, ¹⁰( ) from their regular classes. In some wards in Tokyo,
school subjects are taught in English, or ¹¹( ) of students' native
languages are provided during the lessons.

B **The following are keywords or phrases from the listening. Look them up in your dictionary and write the meanings.**

1. an opening ceremony _____
2. physical education _____
3. Ukrainian _____
4. the Ministry of Education _____
   正式名 (the Ministry of Education, Culture, Sports, Science and Technology)
5. Tagalog _____
6. a ward _____

C **Talk about these pictures and check your understanding of the listening.**

1.
2.
3.

A What do you think?

How can we engage with people from other countries in meaningful, positive ways?

Your answer: _____

•Passage 1 **Title (**)

How did the COVID-19 pandemic impact foreign students who were coming to Japan? In 2021, 150,000 foreign students had obtained residency status but were unable to enter Japan when new entries were completely suspended. Furthermore, this restriction forced many of them to choose other
5 countries as study destinations. According to the Japan Student Services Organization, the number of international students studying in Japan reached around 310,000 in 2019, but dropped to 242,000 in 2021. The government decided to ease the restriction in 2022 by not limiting the number of foreign students coming to Japan.

•Passage 2 **Title (**)

10 The COVID-19 pandemic had a tremendous impact on human interaction around the world, damaging the global economy and globalization efforts. Supply chains were disrupted, and the risks of overseas production were revealed. For example, the COVID-19 pandemic forced people to work and stay at home and increased the demand for semiconductors, essential for PCs and
15 home appliances. Semiconductor factories in Korea and Taiwan could not meet the demand, causing Japanese consumers to wait to actually obtain PCs and home appliances for several months. Furthermore, globalization efforts were also stalled during this time as the pandemic pushed countries to become more nationalistic. They focused on protecting their own citizens, and closed borders
20 to people from other countries.

•Passage 3 **Title (**)

Despite global restrictions necessitated by the COVID-19 pandemic, human activity continued. In Japan, the Immigration Control and Refugee Recognition Act was revised to accept more overseas workers in 2018, and although the rate slowed down, their numbers still increased from 1.65 million in 2019 to 1.72
25 million in 2020. The number of corporations hiring overseas workers also increased, and the resulting cross-cultural workstyle made personnel management for overseas staff an essential part of many organizations. Rakuten, for example, had workers from over 70 countries and promoted using English as a common language. They trained leaders of a group which consists of workers from
30 different countries, using a study of multicultural management as a guide.

B Choose a good title for each passage from the choices below.

1. Multicultural understanding in the workplace   **2.** Globalization

3. The impact of COVID-19 on economy and globalization

4. Global restrictions   **5.** Foreign students

6. The impact of COVID-19 on foreign students studying in Japan

C Fill in the blanks and write an outline for each passage.

•Passage 1

  I. _____

    A. In 2021, 150,000 foreign students were _____ to enter Japan due to restrictions.

    B. The number of international students studying in Japan reached around _____ in 2019, but dropped to _____ in 2021.

    C. The government decided to ease the restriction in 2022.

•Passage 2

  I. _____

    A. Supply chains were disrupted, and the risks of _____ were revealed.

    B. Globalization efforts were stalled during this time as the pandemic pushed countries to become more _____.

•Passage 3

  I. _____

    A. Despite restrictions resulting from the COVID-19 pandemic, _____ continued.

    B. The number of overseas workers in Japan has increased.

    C. The number of corporations _____ overseas workers also has increased.

    D. The resulting cross-cultural workstyle made personnel management for overseas staff an _____ of many organizations.

D Comprehension questions

1. What did the restriction of entries force foreign students to do?

_____

2. What does "nationalistic" mean in this passage?

_____

3. What did Rakuten do regarding multicultural management?

_____

Key phrases

A Use the following key phrases and translate Japanese sentences into English.

例文 1

~ reached around 310,000 in 2019, but dropped to 242,000 in 2021.

Question

この町の人口は、2019 年には 5,000 人になったが、2021 年には 3,000 人まで下がった。

Answer

例文 2

Semiconductor factories in Korea and Taiwan could not meet the demand, causing Japanese consumers to wait to actually obtain PCs and home appliances for several months.

Question

鶏肉が需要に追い付かず、それで鶏肉が高くなった。

Answer

例文 3

~the Immigration Control and Refugee Recognition Act was revised to accept more overseas workers in 2018, ~

Question

今年、外国人労働者が適切なビザで働けるように、法の改正が行われた。

Answer

Data

🔊 2-33

A Study the figure and fill in the blanks.

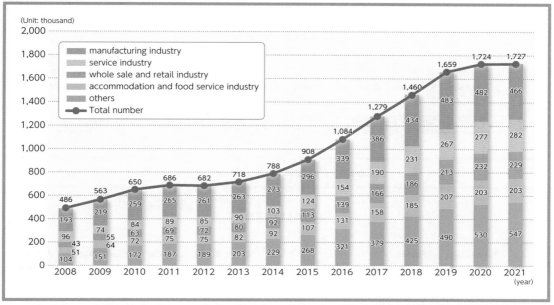

Figure 1. Changes in the Number of Foreign Workers by Industry

Source: the Ministry of Health, Labor and Welfare (厚生労働省)「外国人雇用状況の届出状況」より作成
https://www.mhlw.go.jp/content/11601000/000892808.pdf

Figure 1 shows changes in the number of foreign workers in Japan by $_1$_____.
The source is $_2$_____
_____. The vertical axis indicates the number of workers, in units of $_3$_____.
The horizontal axis shows years from 2008 to 2021.

Compared to 2008, the number of workers in 2021 more than tripled, from $_5$
486,000 to 1,727,000. Throughout these years, the highest number of foreign workers
was found in the $_4$_____ industry. Even in 2021, their number was around
$_5$_____, accounting for 26.9% of the total number of foreign workers. Next were
service industry workers, who numbered 282,000, and accounted for $_6$_____%.

From $_7$_____ to 2019, the total number of foreign workers $_8$_____ sharply. $_{10}$
However, the number of workers in manufacturing $_9$_____ from 2019 to 2021,
which was probably caused by the COVID-19 pandemic.

B Study the figures and fill in the blanks.

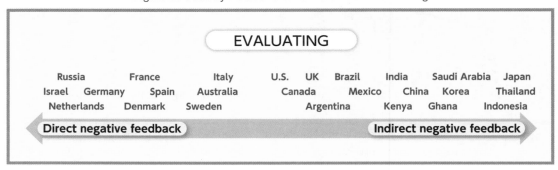

COMMUNICATING

U.S.	Netherlands		Finland			Spain	Italy	Singapore	Iran		China	Japan
Australia	Germany		Denmark	Poland		Brazil	Mexico	France	India	Kenya		Korea
Canada			UK			Argentina			Russia	Saudi Arabia		Indonesia

Low Context ← → **High Context**

Figure 2. Country Positions in Terms of Communicating

EVALUATING

Russia		France		Italy	U.S.	UK	Brazil	India		Saudi Arabia	Japan
Israel	Germany	Spain	Australia		Canada		Mexico	China	Korea		Thailand
Netherlands	Denmark	Sweden			Argentina			Kenya	Ghana		Indonesia

Direct negative feedback ← → **Indirect negative feedback**

Figure 3. Country Positions in Terms of Evaluating

Source: From "The Culture Map" written by Erin Meyer in 2015, illustrating how and why people behave in certain ways.

1. Figure 2 shows positions of countries in communicating from the perspective of low context and _____.

2. Most English-speaking and northern _____ countries have a _____ context, meaning they primarily communicate using only language.

3. On the other hand, many _____ countries are _____ context, meaning they use techniques such as reading between the lines, body language, and tone of voice to communicate.

4. Figure 3 shows country positions in terms of _____ using direct and indirect negative feedback.

5. In Israel, negative feedback can be conveyed directly and in public.

6. In Japan, if an evaluation is negative, it should be conveyed _____ and privately.

7. Interestingly, the U.S. is in the _____ in evaluating, although low context in _____.

8. This suggests that when giving _____ feedback, the people involved should be considered, along with the environment.

Sharing Your Thoughts

A What do you think?

How can we engage with people from other countries in meaningful, positive ways?

Your answer:

1. _____

2. _____

3. _____

4. _____

B Express your opinion.

2-35

Sample conversation

A: To understand people with different cultures, the easiest way might be to make friends with people from overseas.

B: That's true. These days, you can find such people at school and at work.

A: Furthermore, if you are interested in manga, for example, you can use social media to connect with people from overseas who have the same interest.

B: That's right, and this is a hot topic right now because even Japanese might have opportunities to manage people from different cultures. It's possible that an American, a Russian, a Saudi Arabian, an Italian, and someone from China could all be in a meeting together with someone from Japan.

A: That could make it very challenging to reach any sort of conclusion.

B: Exactly! So as Professor Erin Meyer stated, cultural graphs might be helpful for understanding different ways of thinking and behavior.

A: I agree. And also in Japan, there is a similar book to help managers take leadership and bring out the best in their workers.

自分の意見を言う時のストラテジー

具体的な例を出して、意見を構築しましょう。具体例を入れるのは、話すストラテジーだけでなく、聞き手と「文化的に共通したイメージがない場合」も使えます。そのようなとき、話し手はそれを「考慮して」イメージを「具体的に」伝えることで相手の理解を助けることができます。

If you are interested in manga, for example, ～

It's possible that an American, a Russian, a Saudi Arabian …,

Exercise もし、外国人の部下を持ったら、「なるべく早く報告書を出して」などと言ってはだめです。4月18日3時までにと伝えるべきです。

....

....

Group Research

1. Do some research to find how you can have multicultural exchange. Write your findings in the box below.

	Multicultural exchange	Anything you're (they're) careful of
Yourself		
Your school		
Your local town		

Research what two companies are doing to better understand employees from abroad.

Companies	How many foreign workers are employed in Japan? (How many different countries are they from?)	What efforts are being made to help them?
Rakuten		
Other companies		

2. What did you think about the results of your group's research? Talk and write about them in your group.

UNIT 14 Changing Africa

Introduction

2-36

A Listen to the following news story and fill in the blanks.

Africa has been experiencing rapid change and ¹( ). In Kenya, a
²( ) ( ) called the Standard Gauge Railway runs the same distance as
between Tokyo and Kyoto, providing access to a big ³( ) mall called the
Hub Karen. In Ethiopia, a similar train runs between Djibouti and Addis Ababa, and a
highway passes through the country ⁴( ) meters above sea level. Most adults 5
in Africa now have smartphones and cellphones, even though ⁵( )% of farm areas
have no ⁶( ). They use these devices to access Facebook, play games, or
make phone calls. Notably, because most of them don't have bank accounts, they also
use these devices as a ⁷( ) because they make ⁸( ) transactions easy
to carry out. In the wide, dry fields called savannah, Maasai people have both cows 10
and smartphones, which can be charged using ⁹( ) panels or at small shops in
villages for the equivalent of about 20 yen. Thus, since 2003, ¹⁰( ) has
accelerated in many of these places.

B The following are keywords or phrases from the listening. Look them up in
your dictionary and write the meanings.

1. a bullet train _____
2. above sea level _____
3. farm areas _____
4. bank accounts _____
5. a wallet _____
6. make financial transactions _____
7. charge _____
8. urbanization _____

C Talk about these pictures and check your understanding of the listening.

Entrance to the SGR   Shopping Mall in South Africa

A What do you think?

> There are still many poor people in Africa. If Japanese companies start businesses in Africa, what kinds of things should we consider?

Your answer: _____

●Passage 1 **Title (**)

Between the 1980s and '90s, economic development in Africa almost came to a halt. It was called "the Death of Africa." After oil shocks, the price of oil dropped, and it remained low for two decades. Furthermore, the price of agricultural products also fell. This is because too many agricultural products
5 were produced in Africa, and plantations in Asia and South America were also very productive. As a result, supply exceeded worldwide demand. Furthermore, many African countries were politically unstable after gaining independence. They experienced power struggles, dictatorships, corruption, and civil wars. Around 2003, however, China started buying natural resources to support its
10 economic growth, and investing money in Africa.

●Passage 2 **Title (**)

As of 2019, Africa became the poorest continent in the world. According to the World Bank, one in three Africans (about 422 million people) lived on less than 1.90 USD a day, the minimum per day required to support an adult and called the "international poverty line." In sub-Saharan areas particularly, 41%
15 lived below this line. They were unable to buy enough food and suffered from malnutrition. Furthermore, the water supply system serves only 60-70% of the African population. Drinking and using dirty water is common, which causes a lot of sickness. A lower literacy rate also made it challenging to escape from poverty. In some sub-Saharan countries, for men it was 69%; for women 55%.

●Passage 3 **Title (**)

20 Since 2003, the economy in Africa has been developing very rapidly, making some of its people, cities, and countries rich. They feel that investment is more important than aid. Global companies such as L'Oréal, a French hair care company, Samsung, a South Korean home appliance company, and Johnson & Johnson, an American health product company, have set up many branches and
25 factories. A lot of start-ups have also found it easy to start businesses there because no local businesses existed to claim their rights and interests. For example, tele-medical care services and drone delivery expanded quite rapidly. In fact, 20% of the population of Rwanda uses remote health checkup services and receives blood for transfusion delivered by drone.

B **Choose a good title for each passage from the choices below.**

1. More investment
2. Africa — the poorest continent in the world
3. Businesses by start-ups and global companies
4. The death of Africa
5. Economic development in Africa
6. International poverty line

C **Fill in the blanks and write an outline for each passage.**

•Passage 1

I. _____

    A. Between the 1980s and '90s, economic development came to a halt.

        1. After oil shocks;

           a. The price of _____ dropped.

           b. The price of _____ products fell.

             Supply exceeded worldwide _____.

        2. They were politically _____.

•Passage 2

I. _____

    A. As of 2019, Africa became the poorest continent.

        1. One in three Africans lived on less than _____ USD a day.

        2. In Sub-Saharan areas, _____% lived below this line, suffering from

           _____.

        3. The _____ supply system serves only 60-70% of the African population.

        4. A lower _____ also made it challenging to escape from poverty.

•Passage 3

I. _____

    A. Since _____, the economy in Africa has been developing rapidly.

        1. This made some of its people, cities, and countries _____.

        2. Global companies have set up many branches and _____.

        3. A lot of start-ups have also found it easy to start businesses there.

           a. No local businesses existed to claim their _____ and interests.

D **Comprehension questions**

1. What were three causes for the slow economy in Africa?

   _____

2. What also made it challenging for the poor in Africa to escape from poverty?

   _____

3. Why can start-ups create businesses so easily in Africa?

   _____

Key phrases

A Use the following key phrases and translate the Japanese sentences into English.

例文 1

~ , economic development in Africa almost <u>came to a halt</u>.

Question

その計画は感染者が増えたので、突然中止になった。

Answer

例文 2

~, one in three Africans (about 422 million people) lived on <u>less than</u> 1.90 USD a day, ~

Question

去年、この地域の人々は 1 年に 10 万円未満しか収入がなかった。

  ● 収入を得る：earn

Answer

例文 3

Global companies have <u>set up</u> branches and factories.

Question

あるアフリカの地域では、企業は、ゼロから建物とシステムの両方を作らなければならない。

  ● ゼロから：from scratch

Answer

Data

 2-40

A Study the figure and fill in the blanks.

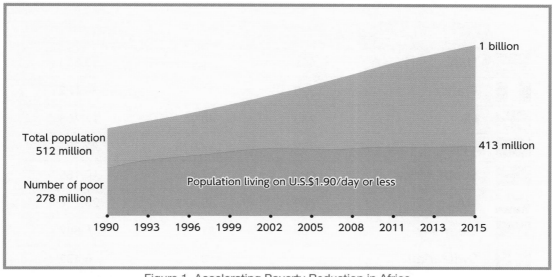

Figure 1. Accelerating Poverty Reduction in Africa

Source: World Bank PovcalNet.
https://www.worldbank.org/en/region/afr/publication/accelerating-poverty-reduction-in-africa-in-five-charts

Figure 1 shows $_1$_____ in Africa. The source of this graph is $_2$_____. The orange section shows the number of $_3$_____ while the blue section shows the $_4$_____ _____. The horizontal axis shows the years from 1990 to 2015. In 1990, the total population was $_5$_____ million while the number of poor was $_6$_____ million. This means that 54% of people live in extreme poverty. This exterme poverty means the population living on $_7$_____.

In 2015, the total population was 1 billion and the number of poor was 413 million. This means that $_8$_____% of people live in extreme poverty. Thus, it can be said that the rates of extreme poverty in Africa have fallen. However, since the total population has increased from 512 million in 1990 to 1 billion in 2015, the actual number of people living in poverty has $_9$_____, from 278 million in 1990 to $_{10}$_____ million in 2015.

B Study the table and fill in the blanks.

Country	Projects	Jobs created	Capital U.S.$m
USA	463	62,004	30,855
France	329	57,970	34,172
UK	286	40,949	17,768
China	259	137,028	72,235
South Africa	199	21,486	10,185
UAE	189	39,479	25,278
Germany	180	31,562	6,887
Switzerland	143	13,363	6,432
India	134	30,334	5,403
Spain	119	13,837	4,389

Table 1. The Top 10 Countries of the Largest Direct Investment in Africa

FDI 2014-2018 by source
Source: FDI Intelligence and EY Africa Attractiveness Report, 2019. より作成―タイトル変更)
https://www.brookings.edu/blog/africa-in-focus/2019/10/09/figure-of-the-week-foreign-direct-investment-in-africa/
FDI (Foreign Direct Investment) / EY (formerly Ernst & Young)

1. Table 1 shows the _____ in Africa.

2. The source of this table is _____
   _____.

3. The survey was conducted from _____.

4. The vertical lists show the top 10 countries, and the numbers on the right show the
   number of _____ and _____ , and the amount of investment.

5. _____ was the largest investor in terms of total capital, investing _____
   million USD. It was twice the dollar amount of both France and _____.

6. In terms of projects, China ranked _____, so it could be said that they invest a
   large amount of money in each project.

7. As can be seen, _____ is also included. This means that intra-African
   investment also grew as even countries in Africa gained strength economically.

Sharing Your Thoughts

A What do you think?

> There are still many poor people in Africa. If Japanese companies start businesses in Africa, what kinds of things should we consider?

Your answer:

1. _____

2. _____

3. _____

4.
   _____

5.
   _____

B Express your opinion.

 2-42

Sample conversation

A: I heard that Japanese companies left Africa due to the bursting of the economic bubble in the 1990s.

B: That may be one of the reasons why most of us have a fixed image of Africa as nothing but a poor continent and a collection of poor countries.

A: Yes, but now in the 2020s, various types of companies, including car firms and trading companies, have tried to expand their businesses again in Africa.

B: And they not only ship cars, but also car parts to be used in knockdown production. This means they have built factories and created a system for assembling cars there.

A: That's a good idea because they can hire local people as employees.

B: Exactly. Those factories not only create jobs, but also teach valuable skills.

自分の意見を言う時のストラテジー

Not only ～ but also で、話の幅を広げることができます。

Exercise 中古車販売の場合は、インターネットで、日本の会社は日本にあるさまざまな車のモデルも見せることができ、アフリカの顧客と直接コミュニケーションが取れます。

....

....

....

Group Research

1. Do some research to find several companies which do business in Africa.

Companies	L'Oréal	Samsung	Kaneka Corporation
Products			
Sales			
Cities and countries			
The number of employees in Africa			
Any other features			

2. What did you think about the results of your group's research? Talk and write about them in your group.

Helping People Make Better Choices

NUDGE THEORY

Introduction

🔊 2-43

A **Listen to the following news story and fill in the blanks.**

At Oze National Park, which stretches across Fukushima, Tochigi, Gunma, and Niigata prefectures, toilets are in danger of ¹( ) due to a lack of ²( ) from visitors. Many national parks in nature ³( ) areas use donations to cover the costs of ⁴( ) restrooms, but only around 30% of users contributed. To solve this problem, the Oze Preservation Foundation, which looks after the park, launched a project using the so-called nudge theory in March, ⁵( ). The method ⁶( ) people to perform a particular action. The foundation conducted two experiments to compare the effects. In the first, a contribution box was placed at the entrance with a photo of a ⁷( ) child. In the second, two boxes were put side by side at the same place, each with a different photo of park ⁸( ). Visitors were asked to choose which of the pictures they preferred and donate money. The first experiment elicited more donations. Making visitors think they are being ⁹( ) seemed more effective than the method of ¹⁰( ) for scenery.

5

10

B **The following are keywords or phrases from the listening. Look them up in your dictionary and write the meanings.**

1. national park _____
2. in danger of _____
3. restrooms _____
4. contribute _____
5. nudge _____
6. scenery _____
7. effective _____

C **Talk about these pictures and check your understanding of the listening.**

1.

2.

3.

A What do you think?

> Do nudges benefit our daily lives?

Your answer: _____

•Passage 1 **Title (   )**

A nudge is a concept in behavioral economics. It was popularized in 2008 by two American scholars, Richard Thaler and Cass Sunstein. It is a way to encourage people to make better decisions. For example, putting fruit at eye level or near the cash register is a nudge to get people to choose healthier food.
5 An essential part of nudges is that they do not involve forcing people to make decisions. Therefore, banning junk food is not a nudge, nor is punishing people for choosing unhealthy food. Thaler says, "If you want people to do something, make it easy." Now in various countries including Japan, organizations called "nudge units" apply nudge theory to public policy.

•Passage 2 **Title (   )**

10 Japan's Ministry of the Environment has been testing a new nudge policy since 2017 with the purpose of reducing CO_2 emissions from households and businesses. For example, it uses neighborhood electricity consumption data in electricity bills. Consumers can compare their own electricity consumption with that of their neighbors and be motivated to reduce their consumption. The
15 ministry took the lead in setting up what it calls a nudge unit in April 2017, involving collaboration from industry, academia, and the public sector. As one example of their work, Oracle Japan and Jukankyo Research Institute Inc. are jointly developing a Japanese-style nudge model by using the above method. The ministry is looking at its applicability to realize a low carbon society.

•Passage 3 **Title (   )**

20 A sludge is essentially the opposite of a nudge. While nudges try to push people to make better decisions by making certain choices easier than others, sludges make a process more difficult with the goal of creating friction, which makes the consumer less likely to continue the process. For example, when you subscribe to a service, the process is easy to complete. In contrast, if you want to
25 cancel a subscription, you have to go through a more difficult and complicated process. Often, canceling requires a phone call, during which you have to explain why you want to cancel, while the operator tries to convince you not to do it. This intentional technique is known as a sludge.

B Choose a good title for each passage from the choices below.

1. Making it easy   **2.** What is a sludge?   **3.** Japan's nudge unit

4. A low-carbon society   **5.** What is a nudge?   **6.** Making difficult decisions

C Fill in the blanks and write an outline for each passage.

•Passage 1

I. _____
- A. a concept in behavioral economics
  - 1. popularized in _____
  - 2. two American scholars, _____ and Cass Sunstein
  - 3. a way to encourage people to make _____
- B. an example
  - 1. putting fruit at _____ or near the _____
  - 2. get people to choose _____ food
  - 3. people are not _____ to make the decision

•Passage 2

I. _____
- A. purpose
  - 1. reducing _____
  - 2. realizing a _____ society
- B. method
  - 1. using neighborhood _____ data in electricity bills
  - 2. collaboration from _____, academia, and the public sector

•Passage 3

I. _____
- A. the opposite of a nudge
  - 1. making a process more _____
  - 2. creating _____
  - 3. making the consumer less likely to _____ the process

D Comprehension questions

1. What is an essential aspect of nudges?

_____

2. What is the goal of the Japanese-style nudge model?

_____

3. How do sludges make a process more difficult?

_____

A Use the following key phrases and translate the Japanese sentences into English.

例文 1

It is a way to encourage people to <u>make</u> better <u>decisions</u>.

Question

君は自分で決断しなければならない。

Answer

例文 2

The ministry <u>took the lead</u> in setting up what it calls a nudge unit.

Question

政府がその計画の始動の先頭に立った。

Answer

例文 3

When you <u>subscribe to</u> a service, the process is easy to complete.

Question

私は2つの新聞を定期購読している。

Answer

Data

 2-47

A Study the figures and fill in the blanks.

Figure 1. Messages to Nudge People into Reducing Electricity Consumption

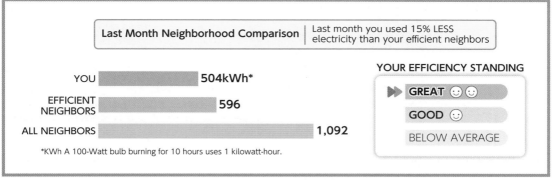

Figure 2. Home Energy Report Letters

Source: FAVEL issues "Urban Nudges II: Using social norms to reduce energy consumption より作成
https://favelissues.com/2014/03/08/urban-nudges-ii-using-social-norms-to-reduce-energy-consumption/

　　Figure 1 shows four different ₁_____ to nudge people into ₂_____ electricity consumption. The experiment was run by a company called Opower in the early 2000s in California. The result showed that only (4) led to a significant reduction of electricity consumption. It nudged people to do as their neighbors do.

　　Figure 2 shows another experiment conducted by the same company, which ₅ involved sending ₃_____ Report Letters to 600,000 families across the U.S. These letters compared the electricity consumption of each ₄_____ to that of their ₅_____. The letter in Figure 2 says, "Last month you used ₆_____ _____ electricity than your ₇_____ neighbors." This program also worked well to reduce ₈_____ consumption. We can learn from the two experiments ₁₀ that people apparently care about their ₉_____ and how their behavior is ₁₀_____ from that of other people.

127

B Study the figure and fill in the blanks.

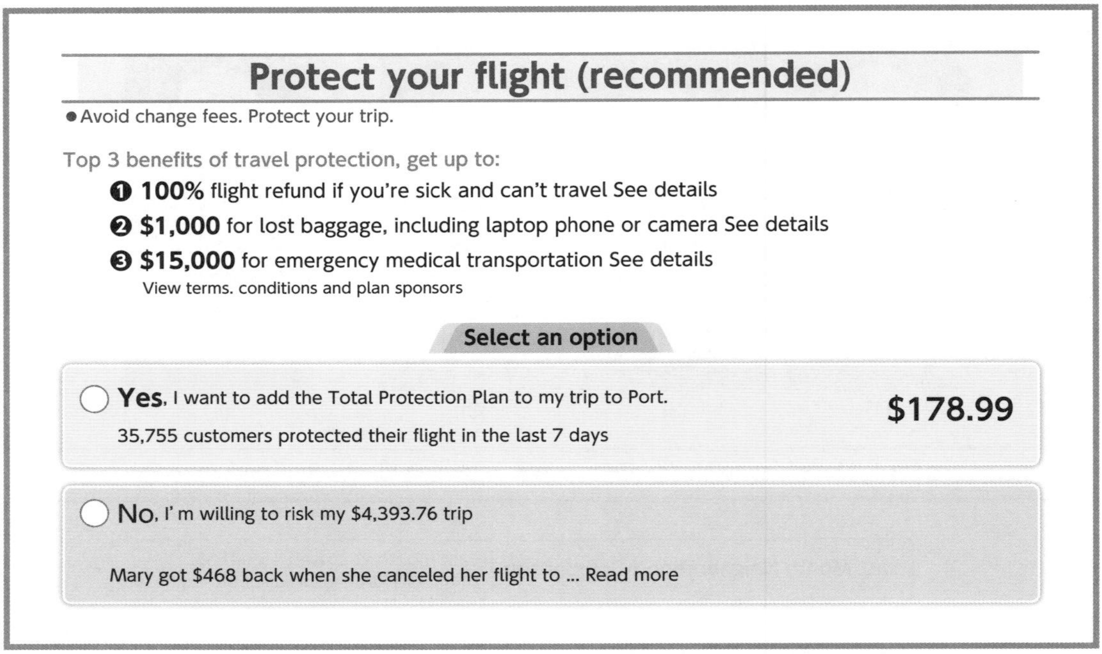

Protect your flight (recommended)

● Avoid change fees. Protect your trip.

Top 3 benefits of travel protection, get up to:
- ❶ **100%** flight refund if you're sick and can't travel See details
- ❷ **$1,000** for lost baggage, including laptop phone or camera See details
- ❸ **$15,000** for emergency medical transportation See details
  View terms. conditions and plan sponsors

Select an option

○ **Yes**, I want to add the Total Protection Plan to my trip to Port.

35,755 customers protected their flight in the last 7 days

$178.99

○ **No**, I'm willing to risk my $4,393.76 trip

Mary got $468 back when she canceled her flight to … Read more

Figure 3. Protect Your Flight (recommended)
Source: IMPACTUALLY "Nudge vs. sludge—the ethics of behavioral interventions" より作成
https://impactually.se/nudge-vs-sludge-the-ethics-of-behavioral-interventions/#

1. The source of Figure 3 is an organization called IMPACTUALLY, where experts in human behavior show examples of _____ and _____.
2. Figure 3 is an example of pre-selected choices of _____ or No that are made for us in an online environment.
3. When we book _____, we are often encouraged to choose an additional _____.
4. The airline booking website nudges us to choose to add _____ _____.
5. Selecting an option is _____.
6. The "Yes" option is _____ and in a bold font.
7. The description "35,755 customers protected their flight" shows many customers _____ the plan.
8. "No, I am willing to risk" makes customers feel they need to _____ their flight.
9. "_____ $468 back" attempts to make customers add the plan without hesitation.

Sharing Your Thoughts

A What do you think?

Do nudges benefit our daily lives?

Your answer:

1. _____

2. _____

3. _____

4. _____

5. _____

B Express your opinion.

 2-49

Sample conversation

A: We learned that there are a lot of nudges around us in our daily lives.

B: Do you think they're beneficial to us?

A: Yes, I do. They encourage us to do the right things, for example, something good for the environment or for our health.

B: I agree, but I hear <u>some nudges can</u> make us do something that we later regret. For example, free trial subscriptions seem beneficial, but you will be automatically charged when the trial period ends. It can be a lot of trouble, so we must be careful.

自分の意見を言う時のストラテジー

断定を避けて可能性を示唆する場合は、主語に some を使い、can, may/might などの助動詞を使って表現することができます。

Some nudges / Some of the nudges can (may / might)...

Exercise ナッジの中には危険性があるものもあります。なぜならそれらは私たちをより良い選択へと導かないかもしれないからです。

....

....

Group Research

1. Do some research to find examples of nudges in other countries. Write your findings in the box below.

Nudge (country)	Photo	Explanation

2. What did you think about the results of your group's research? Talk and write about them in your group.

Useful Expressions

• Giving your opinions

I think that it is a good idea because ～

I don't think that it is a good idea because ～

I agree with this idea because ～

I disagree with this idea because ～

In my opinion, we should/should not do that because ～

My opinion is that we should help them because ～

• Giving your thoughts after research

From the research, I learned that ～

It was interesting to know that ～

I was surprised that ～

I was surprised at/by the fact that ～

The most interesting finding was that ～

The findings of the research will make us ～

Comparing A and B, I found that ～

• Agreeing

I agree with your idea.   I totally agree with you.

I think so, too.

I think you're right.

I feel the same way.

I have no objections.

That's a good idea.

You can say that again.

• Disagreeing

I disagree with your idea.   I disagree with you.

I don't think so.

I don't think that's a good idea.

I have a different opinion.

I'm against it.

I'm opposed to it.

I oppose the idea that ...

That's a good point, but ...

That may be true, but ...

That's one way of looking at it, but ...

• Showing importance

The key point is ...

The important thing here is that ...

• Listing points

The first point is ...   The second point is ...

First, ...   Second, ...   Lastly (Finally), ...

• Giving a cause and effect

... because

..., so

Because of ...

Due to ...

As a result, ...

A results from B.

A results in B.

A leads to B.

Therefore, ...

• Comparison and Contrast

A is like B.

A is the same as B.

A is similar to B.

Also, ...

Likewise, ...

Similarly, ...

A is different from B.

In contrast, ...

On the other hand, ...

..., but ...

...,while ...

• Showing examples

For example, ...

For instance, ...

• Referring to a source

According to an article, ...

The newspaper (A research/ An article) said/showed/ reported that ...

Prof. A suggests/explains/ reports/ states that ...

TEXT PRODUCTION STAFF

edited by	編集
Eiichi Tamura	田村 栄一
Yasutaka Sano	佐野 泰孝

cover design by	表紙デザイン
Nobuyoshi Fujino	藤野 伸芳

text design by	本文デザイン
Hiroyuki Kinouchi (ALIUS)	木野内 宏行 (アリウス)

illustrated by	イラスト
Kyosuke Kuromaru	黒丸 恭介

CD PRODUCTION STAFF

narrated by	吹き込み者
Howard Colefield (AmerE)	ハワード・コールフィールド (アメリカ英語)
Jennifer Okano (AmerE)	ジェニファー・オカノ (アメリカ英語)

CLIL : Discuss the Changing World 2
CLIL : 英語で考える現代社会2

| 2023年1月20日 | 初版発行 |
| 2023年3月30日 | 第3刷発行 |

著　者	仲谷 都　油木田 美由紀
	山崎 勝　Bill Benfield
発 行 者	佐野 英一郎
発 行 所	株式会社 成 美 堂
	〒101-0052　東京都千代田区神田小川町3-22
	TEL 03-3291-2261　FAX 03-3293-5490
	https://www.seibido.co.jp

| 印 刷 | (株)加藤文明社 |
| 製 本 | (株)加藤文明社 |

ISBN 978-4-7919-7268-5　　　　　　　Printed in Japan